# DISPOSITIONS OF LEADERSHIP

Mary:

I really appreciate
your knowledge, insights,
and dedication to
mentoring new principals!

Gary

## PRAISE FOR *DISPOSITIONS OF LEADERSHIP: THE EFFECTS ON STUDENT LEARNING AND SCHOOL CULTURE*

"School leaders who embrace the high goal that every child will grow and learn to their fullest will find this book speaking directly and personally to them. This is no cookbook with limited ingredients and oversimplified methods. It's a guide to the vital inner workings of successful leadership. *Dispositions of Leadership: The Effects on Student Learning and School Culture* reveals how effective leaders think flexibly, interact sensitively, and engage others in the solution of problems. Leadership here is responsive, creative, and adaptive—three essential qualities of the modern school seeking to accommodate the student diversity and demands of an ever-changing world. Practicing principals, teacher leaders, and others will find wisdom here to guide their daily rounds: five dispositions that they can practice and model for others and that can serve as the heart of their own learning and professional growth. This book deserves to be read widely. In its emphasis on networking leaders within and across districts in 'communities of leaders' lies the key to our profession's future success."—Gordon A. Donaldson, Ed.D., professor emeritus of education, University of Maine

"How do we prepare leaders to work in this environment? Adaptability expressed by Heifetz years ago is becoming a necessary skill. By using the dispositions written about in this book, we can adapt our responses by creating a vision, understanding, clarity, and agility. You will find several references to agility, as well as other foundational behaviors. It is knowing the dispositions and having the agility to use when necessary to confront, manage, and move forward in solving to be more successful in an ever-changing world."—William A. Sommers, retired principal, Bricoleur and Leadership coach

"If you could choose one book on the effective practices of the school principal in the 21st century, this is the one! The authors have synthesized salient research in the field of educational leadership and artfully applied it to the implementation of tools and dispositions of the craft. It creates a backdrop for personal reflection, metacognition, and professional growth to become a dynamic leader in our ever-changing world. It is a must-read for all educational leaders from the teacher leader and school principal to district administrator."—Robyn G. Rehmann, principal coach and educational consultant, Anchorage, Alaska

# DISPOSITIONS OF LEADERSHIP

## The Effects on Student Learning and School Culture

**Gary Whiteley**
**Lexie Domaradzki**
**Arthur L. Costa**
**Patricia Muller**

ROWMAN & LITTLEFIELD
Lanham • Boulder • New York • London

Published by Rowman & Littlefield
A wholly owned subsidiary of The Rowman & Littlefield Publishing Group, Inc.
4501 Forbes Boulevard, Suite 200, Lanham, Maryland 20706
www.rowman.com

Unit A, Whitacre Mews, 26-34 Stannary Street, London SE11 4AB

British Library Cataloguing in Publication Information Available

**Library of Congress Cataloging-in-Publication Data**

Names: Whiteley, Gary, 1954– author. | Domaradzki, Lexie, 1959– author. | Costa,
    Arthur L., author.
Title: Dispositions of leadership : the effects on student learning and school culture /
    Gary Whiteley, Lexie Domaradzki, Arthur L. Costa, Patricia Muller.
Description: Lanham : Rowman & Littlefield, a wholly owned subsidiary of The
    Rowman & Littlefield Publishing Group, Inc., [2017] | Includes bibliographical
    references and index.
Identifiers: LCCN 2017016798 (print) | LCCN 2017031684 (ebook) | ISBN
    9781475836271 (electronic) | ISBN 9781475836257 (cloth : alk. paper) | ISBN
    9781475836264 (pbk. : alk. paper)
Subjects: LCSH: Educational leadership—United States. | School management and
    organization—United States. | Learning.
Classification: LCC LB2805 (ebook) | LCC LB2805 .W4776 2017 (print) | DDC
    371.2—dc23
LC record available at https://lccn.loc.gov/2017016798

∞™ The paper used in this publication meets the minimum requirements of
American National Standard for Information Sciences—Permanence of Paper
for Printed Library Materials, ANSI/NISO Z39.48-1992.

Printed in the United States of America

*To all those hardworking educators who use their energies, talent, and knowledge to facilitate others' continuous and deepened learning. Through their efforts, the world is becoming a more thoughtful, empathic, and loving place.*

# CONTENTS

# FIGURES, TABLES, AND TEXTBOXES

## FIGURES

## TABLES

## TEXTBOXES

# FOREWORD

**P**ractitioners and students of educational leadership will treasure this book that redefines what it takes to lead public schools in the twenty-first century. Describing the century-long journey that has shaped educational leadership, the authors focus on extensive research and personal experience to create a landmark definition of what it takes to be an educational leader with the responsibility and ability to affect student learning. This relationship to student learning is one of two aspects in which this book stands apart from others. The second is the authors' description of developing leadership dispositions, attributes that go beyond knowledge or abilities to what leaders are apt to do. Dispositions are acquired, they say, not in graduate schools but in the interactions between skillful thinking and circumstances that lack solution algorithms. Rather, the agile educational leader relies on maps of the territory and honed habits of intelligent responses to the unusual.

Describing educational leadership as a domain of its own, apart from business, industrial, or entrepreneurial leadership from which it has often borrowed principles and practices, *educational leadership* in this book stands alone as unique, adaptive, and advanced enough to suit this era of extraordinary complexity.

At once practical, grounded in research and vision, the authors frame the necessary requirements for educational leadership today. Educational leaders, this book asserts, must develop adaptive competence to lead learning in the information age. This book takes the reader beyond the traditional command-and-control models that are no longer capable of providing the necessary flexibility to adapt and thrive in today's complex learning environments. Their vision, based on extensive research, the neurosciences, and management literature, casts an effective *educational leader* as adaptive, responsive, agile, and self-aware and a conscientious seeker of continuous learning for self and others. Adaptive competency characterizes such leaders.

Ho-hum was my attitude as I approached the chapters on dispositions (chapters 4–9). I've spent over thirty years in close association with one of the authors, Art Costa, and know—or thought I knew—his thinking about dispositions. I was pleasantly surprised and eminently pleased to find I was learning new concepts and much practical information that can inform and guide educational leaders. Adult learning, the authors report, is pretty directly influenced by leaders who set up a holding environment in which members feel safe, a condition of psychological safety identified by Google research on effective teams as the most important factor producing effective work (Duhigg 2016).

In their view, the effective leader mindfully develops five leadership dispositions—in a sense, habits or patterns of what they are likely to do. Supported with these internal resources, they teach and model effective interpersonal communication as they organize network-centric collaborative groups capable of intelligently responding to today's educational complexities.

We've arrived at this new chapter in the history of educational leadership based on these premises. Ours is a different model than that practiced in medicine, business, or the military for two reasons. Change occurs in public education through a process of accretion, "an inexact and idiosyncratic change process that gradually places layers upon an existing structure."

The second reason is that the nature of teaching and learning itself has changed from that of the industrial age. Then it was largely teacher-centric and directed from the top. In the information age, teaching needs to be more adaptive, learner-centric, and personalized with learning environments continuously adaptive to address changing realities.

This new model of educational leadership is grounded in the type of agile thinking needed to accommodate and respond to an era of extraordinary complexity and parallels similar interests in medicine, the military, and business. The model embraces a growth mindset, is free from recipe, and is continuously adaptive.

Thinking and acting interdependently, communicating to influence, gathering and applying information for change, seeking support and feedback for learning, and pursuing adaptive competence compose the new curriculum for educational leaders.

This book is timely and needed in this quickly evolving world and belongs in every library, every university class on educational leadership, and in the office and home of aspiring and practicing leaders.

Robert J. Garmston, EdD
Professor Emeritus, Education Administration
California State University, Sacramento California

## REFERENCE

Duhigg, C. (2016). *Smarter faster better: The secrets of being productive in life and business.* New York: Random House.

# PREFACE

School leaders work in a complex world. The challenges faced require a system that is agile and people who are capable of being adaptable. These two qualities coexist when organizational structures are flexible and leadership thinking is dispositional in nature. Our goal in *Dispositions of Leadership: The Effects on Student Learning and School Culture* is to provide both a connection to a substantive research base and examples from practice that school leaders find useful.

We benefited from working in school systems and schools side by side with leaders. Our work has been both providing technical assistance and offering professional-learning opportunities. It is humbling to work in busy schools and observe directly if the technical assistance is impactful and if the leadership thinking, capabilities, and practices are useful. We have sought formative feedback from school leaders and gained insight through extensive program evaluation. In other words, we did not first review the literature and then write the book.

The dance between implementing research-based strategies and compiling practice-based evidence has kept us asking, is this information known to be effective, and how does it translate into practice? We discovered that it would be simpler to write a tome and let the reader figure it out, or develop strategies and processes that do not pass through a filter informed by research and practice. We asked school leaders for formative feedback, and they tended to check a *commonsense* and a *get practical* meter and offer suggestions—many suggestions!

*Dispositions of Leadership: The Effects on Student Learning and School Culture* has over fifty figures, tables, and textboxes. This hefty number, used to provide either a visual for a concept or an example to implement, is enough to drive any publisher or printer a little crazy. We are not certain if this occurred but are certain about the two reasons we provided so many examples. The first reason is principals frequently ask for resources that could be used immediately.

The second reason is inspired by the idea of *nudge* popularized by Richard Thaler and Cass Sunstein (2009). We hear principals report they are overwhelmed by all that is expected and demanded of them. It is difficult to think clearly when many options are presented, or to take the information and translate it into practice. Simple and concrete steps can provide a nudge, a starting point or a way to get started. When the same information presented in the tables is used by colleagues and adapted or improved, a network is created that can support and sustain professional growth.

We hope that you as the reader feel a nudge and continue reading *Dispositions of Leadership: The Effects on Student Learning and School Culture*.

## REFERENCE

Thaler, R., and Sunstein, C. (2009). *Nudge: Improving decisions about health, wealth, and happiness*. New York: Penguin.

# ACKNOWLEDGMENTS

It is with profound gratitude that we thank Gordon Donaldson, Bob Garmston, Russ Quaglia, and David Perkins for their personal friendship and lifelong professional commitment to improving the world through education. It has been humbling to have colleagues provide unconditional support and express their faith in us.

We would like to thank our colleagues who made the Alaska Administrator Coaching Project a learning lab for many of the ideas in *Dispositions of Leadership: The Effects on Student Learning and School Culture*. The tireless commitment to coach early career principals by Carol Kane, Dennis Dunn, Tom Briscoe, Dave Cloud, Sandy Lanning, Ron Keffer, Mick Wykis, Peter Kokes, Jim Gillis, Sandy Hill, Reed Carlson, Randy Swenson, Terry Dunn, and Larry Nauta has been inspirational.

We are indebted to Roger Sampson, former president of the Education Commission of the States, and Les Morse, former deputy commissioner of education for the state of Alaska. Their political skill and personal persistence secured funding for the Alaska Administrator Coaching Project in which so many of the ideas within this book had a home for a decade.

The editorial assistance of Tom Koerner, Susan Canavan, Leigh Kupersmith, and Dan Alpert was invaluable. Our editors were patient, kind, and offered insights and suggestions that truly improved this book.

Finally, a deep sense of love and appreciation is due to our family members—Mary Whiteley, Jill Jolliff, Nancy Costa, and Betty Whitmore. Their support, patience, and encouragement have been unwavering.

# INTRODUCTION

School leadership's function, then, is to mobilize people to change how they themselves work so that they collectively serve the emerging needs of children and the demands of society.

—Gordon A. Donaldson Jr.

The intent of this book is to rethink how schools are led. Traditional approaches often focus either on telling leaders how to think or instead on addressing educators' requests to "just tell me what to do." Approaches that focus on telling leaders how to think are often too abstract and theoretical to be very useful or meaningful. Similarly, a "just tell me what to do" approach that focuses on following standardized processes often falls short given the complexity of today's world.

Complexity, and how to effectively respond to the challenges it presents, is front and center for organizations in the current information age. Business, medicine, education, and the U.S. military are encountering an era where traditional, formal, and command-and-control models of leadership are in need of revision. Educational organizations need new mental models and new thinking in the face of this complexity. These mental models, schema, and metaphors will ultimately shape how educators view and think about complex problems.

This book provides a coherent framework for addressing this complexity by gleaning the best from traditional formal organizational thinking, as well as the existing research linking leadership with student learning. This book presents a new model of educational leadership developed by the authors—a model that is grounded in the type of agile thinking needed to accommodate and respond to an era of extraordinary complexity. The model provides school leaders and other educators with a comprehensive framework and corresponding set of tools to draw upon to effectively lead within the complex environments of today's schools.

## COMPLEXITY OF THE CONTEMPORARY EDUCATIONAL SYSTEM

Dr. Murray Gell-Mann, who was awarded the Nobel Prize in Physics in 1969, studied the nature of complexity and Complex Adaptive Systems (CAS). Gell-Mann (1995–1996) traced the meaning of complexity to the Latin root words of *plexus* and *complexus*. *Plexus* means braided or entwined. *Complexus* means braided together. Complexity is, by definition, the intricate intertwining of elements within a system, or between a system and its environment. The challenges of complexity cross disciplinary boundaries, such as biology, computer science, physics, economics, and education.

The implications of recent developments in cognitive science research about how children learn, the effective strategies used to teach, and how teachers make decisions minute by minute in their classrooms are examples of complexity. Current formal organizations, with hierarchical structures designed in an earlier era, are not equipped to solve emerging problems that are very complex, such as those emerging in the twenty-first and twenty-second centuries.

The contemporary education system in the United States has developed a unique set of attributes that distinguishes it from business and industry. Educating children and young adults is different from managing a small business, running a corporation, or providing health-care services. Students, parents, and teachers are not customers, patients, or clients. In addition, while success in business may be measured in terms of profits and losses, negotiating more franchises, or obtaining more patents, aspects of education are difficult to measure in terms of significance to students, learning, and the future world.

Wise educational leaders draw upon the principles, practices, knowledge, and history gleaned from the worlds of business and industry. However, when situations are played out in the unique arenas of the classroom, school, or educational community, the principles and practices of business and industry come up short because of the complexity of schooling (Kirp 2014). Attributes that contribute to the complexity of the contemporary educational system include the following:

- The education system of the United States has the responsibility for educating youth for at least a twelve-to-thirteen-year duration.
- Contemporary schools serve diverse and often disparate purposes, with schools responsible for teaching, assessing, and reporting on learners' ability and inclination to read and compute to function successfully as citizens in a democracy; to be prepared for careers and college; to serve as contributing members of an immediate community and a larger society; to be technologically literate; to know how to work independently and collaboratively; and to have the disposition to continue learning throughout their lifetime.
- Schools are governed by multiple levels of bureaucracy, including school, school district, school board, state, and federal leadership. For most of these levels beyond schools and school districts, participants change approximately every four years, so are thus subject to the political views of a changing slate of legislators and policy makers.
- Since all the public has experienced schooling, each parent, voter, and critic has strong and divergent philosophical convictions about what education should be.
- Leaders are expected to reform school practices in response to and in relation to the learning needs of society and the rapid advances of technology. Examples of challenges include ambitious curriculum goals, accountability for standardized test results, a variety of physical and online classroom materials, new technology devices, heterogeneous classrooms, cultural diversity, an increasing emphasis on "noncognitive" learning, individual education plans, learning specialists, external service agencies, tutoring, summer school, teacher evaluation rubrics, instructional coaches, and more (Bryk 2015).
- Public schools are the only institutions held accountable for educating all children regardless of their diversity of race, culture, language, level of poverty or affluence, mental or physical health, and degree of parental influence.
- Achieving quality outcomes reliably in such complex systems as schools requires a distinctive method of inquiry. It is not known whether any change introduced will actually lead to improvement or if it might produce unintended negative consequences (Bryk 2015).

This uniquely complex nature of the contemporary educational system means that teaching and learning are being redefined. The emerging evidence about how students learn, and how teachers teach, is so dynamic that educators must continually recalibrate their teaching and hone their practice just to keep up with the latest scientific knowledge. These challenges facing contemporary leaders require an understanding of these complexities in the current system, as well as an understanding of how to accommodate the changing nature of work and learning in the twenty-first century.

## WHY ARE NEW UNDERSTANDINGS OF EDUCATIONAL LEADERSHIP NEEDED?

Adjustments are needed in both thinking and structure to accommodate the contemporary world of work and learning that is significantly different from those established by formal organizations and designed for the industrial age. Frank Levy and Richard Murnane (2004) note that the tasks carried out by the American workforce from 1969 to 1998 indicate a steady decline of routine manual and cognitive tasks and an increase in expert thinking and complex communication, as noted in figure 0.1.

Figure 0.1 depicts two concepts: expert thinking and complex communication. *Expert thinking* is the ability to solve new or novel problems that cannot be solved by the simple application of rules. *Complex communication* is the ability to communicate information from multiple sources of data

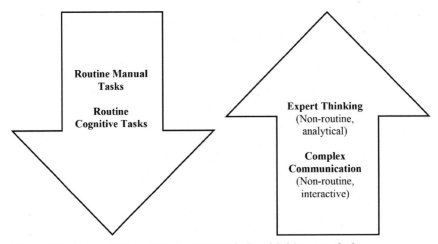

**Figure 0.1.   The shift in task output and the thinking needed**

and simultaneously convey accurately an interpretation to others. Expert thinking and complex communication are nonroutine and require an approach that involves both adaptability and flexibility.

The educational system will need to incorporate these changes in the nature of work and learning in the twenty-first century by integrating expert thinking and complex communication into how schools are led, the ways teachers instruct and interact with one another, and the ways students learn. In this current educational environment, a school leader, teacher, or learner will need to extrapolate information from multiple sources, apply the knowledge in novel or nonroutine settings, and utilize appropriate cultural interpersonal skills in order to communicate with peers (Schleicher 2007).

## LEARNING ENVIRONMENTS AND THE NEED FOR ADAPTIVE COMPETENCE

These changes in the nature of work and learning have been accompanied by a renewed focus on insights into human learning during the past decade. Optimal learning environments are best appreciated as a complex human endeavor rather than being viewed simplistically or reduced to a series of isolated practices. As Hanna Dumont, David Istance, and Francisco Benavides suggest, "Learning balances the acquisition of concepts, skills, and meta-cognitive competencies" (2010, 75).

A learning environment considers the integration of the inseparable components of content acquisition, knowledge application, motivation, effort, persistence, self-efficacy, and metacognition. In addition, learning is a process that simultaneously combines cognition with emotion, with learning environments increasingly viewed as collaborative and social by nature. This understanding of learning requires interpersonal capabilities such as listening, self-regulation, and skillful interactions within a group to achieve an optimal learning environment.

This understanding of learning and learning environments also intrinsically requires learners to combine metacognitive strategies with previously learned content knowledge simultaneously. In fact, many scholars who investigate the nature of learning agree that adaptive competence is an ultimate goal of learning (Bransford et al. 2006; de Corte 2010). *Adaptive competence* is the ability to flexibly and creatively apply domain-specific knowledge and utilize metacognitive strategies that were acquired from formal and informal learning situations and apply them in novel or nonroutine settings.

Adaptive competence as an ultimate goal of learning does not make the acquisition of foundation skills in a systematic manner less important. Adaptive competence is only possible when a solid foundation of content knowledge and skills is at the disposal of a learner. However, it is important to remember that learning can be demanding and stressful, and many learners need to have the capacity to manage their emotions.

Learning environments that promote adaptive competence create circumstances whereby learners (including students, teachers, and school leaders) are vulnerable because it might reveal that they do not know what to do. When learners do not know how to move forward, and are cognitively overloaded or frustrated, they need positive beliefs about themselves and strategies to utilize.

## HABITS OF MIND OR DISPOSITIONS

Habits of mind or dispositions become necessary in learning environments that require adaptive thinking. *Habits of mind* means knowing how to behave intelligently when you do not know the answer. Habits of mind also means having a disposition toward behaving intelligently when confronted with problems to which the answers are not immediately known. Complex environments present numerous situations in which the answers are not immediately known.

These habits of mind are a composite of many skills, attitudes, and proclivities. Table 0.1 identifies the sixteen habits of mind and provides a brief description of each. Arthur Costa and Bena Kallick (2008), who have worked for several decades with habits of mind, note that these dispositions are an integral part of learning. These authors also note that habits of mind are as important to learning as specific content knowledge.

Earlier in the introduction it was noted that changes in the nature of work and learning require educational systems to integrate expert thinking and complex communication into how schools are led, the ways teachers instruct and interact with one another, and the ways students learn. These habits of mind or dispositions are needed to exhibit expert thinking and complex communication by students, teachers, or school leaders. Expert thinking is enhanced by the following subset of habits of mind or dispositions:

- Managing impulsivity
- Thinking and communicating with clarity and precision

**Table 0.1.  Habits of mind or dispositions**

| | Habits of mind (dispositions) | Description |
|---|---|---|
| 1 | Listening with understanding and empathy | Devoting mental energy to another person's thoughts and ideas; making an effort to perceive another's point of view and emotions |
| 2 | Managing impulsivity | Thinking before acting; remaining calm, thoughtful, and deliberative |
| 3 | Thinking and communicating with clarity and precision | Striving for accurate communication in both written and oral form; avoiding overgeneralizations, distortions, deletions, and exaggerations |
| 4 | Thinking and acting interdependently | Being able to work with and learn from others in reciprocal situations; teamwork |
| 5 | Thinking about your thinking (metacognition) | Being aware of your own thoughts, strategies, feelings, and actions and their effects on others |
| 6 | Applying past knowledge to new situations | Accessing prior knowledge; transferring knowledge beyond the situation in which it was learned |
| 7 | Striving for accuracy | Always doing your best; setting high standards; checking and finding ways to improve constantly; searching for truth |
| 8 | Creating, imagining, and innovating | Generating new and novel ideas, fluency, and originality |
| 9 | Thinking flexibly | Being open minded, being able to change perspectives, generating alternatives, and considering options |
| 10 | Remaining open to continuous learning | Having humility and pride when admitting we don't know; resisting complacency |
| 11 | Persisting | Persevering on a task through to completion; remaining focused; looking for ways to reach your goal when stuck; not giving up |
| 12 | Questioning and problem posing | Having a questioning attitude; knowing what data are needed and developing questioning strategies to produce those data; finding problems to solve |
| 13 | Gathering data through all senses | Paying attention to the world around you; gathering data through all the senses: taste, touch, smell, hearing, and sight |
| 14 | Responding with wonderment and awe | Finding the world awesome and mysterious, and being intrigued with phenomena and beauty |
| 15 | Finding humor | Finding the whimsical, incongruous, and unexpected; being able to laugh at oneself |
| 16 | Taking responsible risks | Being adventuresome; living on the edge of one's competence; trying new things constantly |

Source: Costa, A. L., and Kallick, B. (2008). *Learning and leading with habits of mind: 16 essential characteristics for success.* Alexandria, VA: Association for Supervision and Curriculum Development.

- Thinking about your thinking (metacognition)
- Applying past knowledge to new situations
- Striving for accuracy
- Creating, imagining, and innovating; thinking flexibly
- Remaining open to continuous learning
- Persisting

Complex communication is enhanced by the habits of mind or dispositions that focus on interpersonal skills:

- Thinking and communicating with clarity and precision
- Listening with understanding and empathy
- Thinking and acting interdependently by working with and learning from others

Therefore, learning environments that incorporate expert thinking, complex communication, and habits of mind or dispositions are more likely to promote adaptive competence. As depicted in figure 0.2, the trilogy of expert thinking, complex communication, and dispositions are integral to

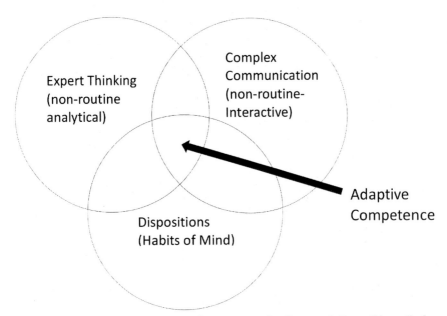

**Figure 0.2. Expert thinking, complex communication, and dispositions (habits of mind)**

promoting the types of adaptive competence needed in twenty-first-century educational leadership.

## EDUCATIONAL LEADERSHIP IN THE INFORMATION AGE

As society experiences a paradigm shift from the industrial age to the information age, there is no simple formula for how school systems and schools accommodate the past while simultaneously providing leaders with the preparation needed to embrace an unknown future. What is known, however, is that the models of leadership designed in the industrial age, such as the heroic leader, are in need of revision.

Despite a plethora of leadership styles, theories, and principles that have been advocated across the years, the field of education still lacks a framework that provides educators with the type of coherent system of thinking that is needed to lead school systems and schools in the complexity of today's environment. This book proposes new vocabulary and patterns of thinking about distributive leadership and adaptive competencies, rather than a list of things leaders are supposed to do within their schools. These dispositions and patterns of thinking are intended to provide principals and teachers with a tool set to draw upon within complex environments.

The core of the framework described in this book focuses on dispositions of contemporary educational leadership that are needed to ensure that educators and students flourish in the twenty-first century: thinking and acting interdependently, communicating to influence, gathering and applying information for change, seeking support and feedback for learning, and pursuing adaptive competence. These five dispositions act as a schema for developing mental models that assist leaders when they encounter the ambiguity of many complex problems.

However, as depicted in figure 0.3, these dispositions need to be supported by a strong foundational understanding of the effect of educational leadership on student learning. This foundational understanding will help to provide needed focus and clarity to school leaders' work. In addition, as depicted in the figure, successfully activating these dispositions also requires a foundational understanding of agile organizational structures. This new schema will provide educators with the flexibility needed to lead in complex learning environments and to effectively address adaptive challenges within the contemporary school system.

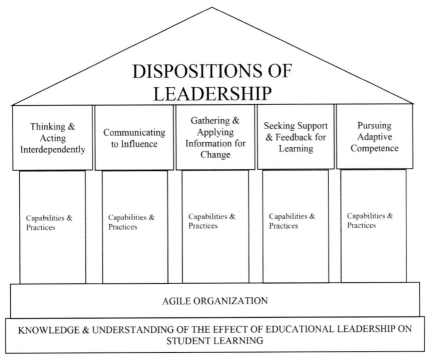

**Figure 0.3. Dispositions of leadership framework**

## OVERVIEW OF THE BOOK

The remainder of this book focuses on providing the knowledge, understanding, and tools needed in each of these three areas of the proposed framework for effective school leadership in the information age:

- Effects of educational leadership on student learning (chapter 1)
- Organizational structure needed to support school leadership (chapter 2)
- Importance of dispositions for contemporary educational leadership (chapter 3) and how to activate dispositional thinking (chapters 4 through 8)

First, new and practical concepts for leading schools are needed that draw upon the extensive research focused on leading and student learning. Chapter 1 provides an overview of the century-long evolution of educational leadership needed to understand the difficulties of changing leadership structures and practices, as well as describing the new era of leadership with student learning as a pervasive focus. Successful schools have effective principals, and they recognize that leadership is not limited to an individual in a formal role.

Second, the work of improving schools requires that change happens within the organization and individuals simultaneously. Chapter 2 provides an overview of the current formal organization, which relies on bureaucratic procedures and structures, and describes agile organizations and network-centric groups to address the adaptive challenges within the contemporary school system. Leadership in school districts and schools in the information age will need to distribute dispositions, capabilities, and practices throughout the organization because deeper levels of learning will be expected.

Third, the book describes a model of educational leadership that places these key elements of understanding the effects of educational leadership on student learning, and knowledge of organizational structures to support school leadership, as the foundation upon which dispositional thinking can be activated for effective educational leadership in the information age. Chapter 3 describes the importance of dispositions for contemporary educational leadership and discusses how to activate dispositional thinking.

In particular, five dispositions of leadership are presented as critical for school leadership in the information age. Chapters 4 through 8 discuss these five dispositions of leadership:

- Thinking and acting interdependently (chapter 4)
- Communicating to influence (chapter 5)
- Gathering and applying information for change (chapter 6)
- Seeking support and feedback for learning (chapter 7)
- Pursuing adaptive competence (chapter 8)

These five dispositions of leadership have been designed to play a role in preparing early career school leaders and providing ongoing professional learning for experienced school leaders. These dispositions can also assist in hiring and in assessing leadership effectiveness. A powerful use of the dispositions of leadership is through school-district-created, high-performing teams of school leaders. Increasingly, accountability should rely less on external consequences and more on an ongoing and systematic approach of support and feedback that values a focus on both student learning and retaining effective leaders.

Finally, the book concludes by describing how the overall model of educational leadership presented in this book can help leaders who have been searching for effective ways to address complex problems and improve the learning environment for all students. The final chapter (chapter 9) notes how the model consisting of the five dispositions of leadership, grounded in a foundational understanding of the effects of educational leadership on both student learning and agile organizations, can also

- serve as lenses and filters for observing, understanding, diagnosing, and strengthening organizational conditions;
- foster learning of staff members; and
- contribute to one's own self-discovery.

The final chapter describes the positive effects that may be observed on organizational culture, the staff and students, and the school leader, as the dispositions of leadership become more apparent. In addition, a detailed vignette is presented that illustrates the application of the capabilities drawn from the five dispositions of leadership.

## QUESTIONS TO ENGAGE YOUR THINKING AND DISCUSSION WITH COLLEAGUES

1. What practices have you observed within your organization that promote expert thinking, complex communication, and use of dispositions?
2. As you apply concepts from this chapter, what makes educational leadership uniquely complex in your setting?

## REFERENCES

Bransford, J., Stevens, R., Schwartz, D., Meltzoff, A., Pea, R., Roschelle, J., and Sabelli, N. (2006). Learning theories and education: Toward a decade of synergy. In P. A. Alexander and P. H. Winne (Eds.), *Handbook of educational psychology* (2nd ed., pp. 209–244). Mahwah, NJ: Erlbaum.
Bryk, A. (2015, December). Accelerating how we learn to improve. *Educational Researcher, 44*(89), 467–477.
Costa, A. L., and Kallick, B. (2008). *Learning and leading with habits of mind: 16 essential characteristics for success.* Alexandria, VA: Association for Supervision and Curriculum Development.
de Corte, E. (2010). Historical developments in the understanding of learning. In H. Dumont, D. Istance, and F. Benavides (Eds.), *The nature of learning: Using*

*research to inspire practice* (pp. 35–67). Paris: Organisation for Economic Co-operation and Development, Innovative Learning Environments Project.

Dumont, H., Istance, D., and Benavides F. (Eds.). (2010). *The nature of learning: Using research to inspire practice*. Paris: Organisation for Economic Co-operation and Development, Innovative Learning Environments Project.

Gell-Mann, M. (1995–1996). Let's call it plectics. *Complexity, 1*(5). Retrieved from http://tuvalu.santafe.edu/.

Kirp, D. L. (2014, August 16). Teaching is not a business. *New York Times*, Sunday Review Opinion. Retrieved from http://www.nytimes.com/.

Levy, F., and Murnane, R. (2004). *The new division of labor: How computers are creating the next job market*. Princeton, NJ: Princeton University Press.

Schleicher, A. (2007). Science competencies for tomorrow's world: Seeing school systems through the prism of PISA. PowerPoint slides. Retrieved from www.oecd.org/unitedstates/39773685.ppt.

**1**

# WHAT EFFECT DOES EDUCATIONAL LEADERSHIP HAVE ON STUDENT LEARNING?

It is not particularly fruitful to ask whether leaders make a difference to student learning or achievement because the answer depends on what they actually do.

—Viviane Robinson, *Student-Centered Leadership* (2011, 143)

**N**ew and practical concepts for leading schools are needed that draw upon the extensive body of research focused on leading and student learning. Prior research on leadership in education generally lacked a body of evidence to support the work of district-level or school-level leaders. However, for the first time, recent research findings by two groups of researchers led by Viviane Robinson and Kenneth Leithwood have established a solid, research-based foundation for educational leadership at the school level.

The term *educational leadership* is used in this book to suggest a transition away from *leadership in education* and the historical borrowing from other professions and disciplines. Robinson and Leithwood, with their respective colleagues, identified linkages between leadership capabilities and student learning that help to form the foundation for educational leadership in the twenty-first century. Therefore, this chapter explores these recent research findings to provide a much deeper understanding of the link between school leadership and student learning.

In addition, however, it is important to have an understanding of historical inheritance, especially to address questions such as, Why is school leadership the way it is? And why is changing leadership structure and practice so challenging? The foundation of leadership in education as a field of study is based upon theories, philosophies, and frameworks borrowed from sociology, social psychology, economics, anthropology, political science, the military, and business management.

Although leadership in education is a relatively young field of study, many theorists and authors have provided important elements that advanced the field's understanding of leadership. Therefore, before discussing the more recent research findings linking school leadership and student learning, this chapter first examines key contributions that have influenced current understanding of educational leadership. This chapter provides an overview of the evolution of educational leadership, noting twenty-five significant books from 1911 through 2013 that illustrate the relatively slow development of leadership in education as a field of study.

## THE CENTURY-LONG EVOLUTION OF EDUCATIONAL LEADERSHIP

David Tyack and Elizabeth Hansot, in *Managers of Virtue: Public School Leadership in America, 1820–1980* (1982), made an important observation: "One reason schools have been able to absorb outside demands for change is that they have been steadily expanding during most of their history and could reform by accretion" (11). Accretion is an idiosyncratic change process that gradually places layers upon an existing structure so that the entire fabric becomes a composite of all the layers added. Thus, philosophies and theories from numerous disciplines, appropriate for various historical periods, are layered upon the canvas of educational leadership.

Sydney Alhstrom, in *A Religious History of the American People* (2004), suggests that Americans tend to be "ahistorical" and "present-minded" when it comes to having an understanding of the past. The five tables in this chapter provide a brief sampling of the past one hundred years of literature and illustrate many of the practices that contributed to the foundation of educational leadership. Scholars have written extensively about leadership, and this brief look at the literature is not intended to be exhaustive. Many fine books and authors were not included since the intent is a brief overview that is illustrative and not an extensive literature compilation.

## TWENTY-FIVE IMPORTANT WORKS IN FIVE TABLES

The literature noted in tables 1.1 to 1.5 reveals the evolution of thinking by theorists and practitioners, from making sense of leadership in the industrial age to models and philosophies that accommodate the complexity of the information age. Selected authors who have researched teaching and learning are also included in order to not separate educational leadership from student learning. The linking of leadership capacities and practices to student learning is what distinguishes educational leadership from leadership in other professions.

In his exhaustive review in *Leadership for the Twenty-First Century* (1993), Joseph Rost reminds us that the leadership literature for seventy of the past ninety years is "a critique of the efforts of leadership scholars and practitioners in the twentieth century to understand leadership based on the values and cultural norms of the industrial paradigm" (xiv). He characterizes the mainstream literature on leadership from about 1910 through the 1980s as "overwhelmingly industrial in its concept of leadership" (100). Thus, efficiency, bureaucracy, and the heroic leader are the dominant influences on present conceptions of leadership and a place to begin.

### Efficiency, Bureaucracy, and the Heroic Leader, 1911–1967

School systems are still deeply committed to bureaucracy, efficiency, and command-and-control structures described nearly a century ago. Table 1.1 covers six decades and provides the foundation for leadership, starting with Fredrick Taylor and Max Weber articulating our understanding of bureaucracy, control, centralization, and efficiency. The heroic leader—the ability to persuade and direct men—emerged and was reinforced by two world wars, as illustrated by biographies about famous wartime figures. It was thought that leaders have inherent traits that make them capable of leading.

The roles and needs of followers, for the purpose of establishing shared goals, begin to emerge, but the dominant themes are leader-centric. The managerial grid takes hold, and a contemporary version finds leaders placing themselves into one of four quadrants that contain many adjectives about leadership. Many leaders, past and present, have completed inventories that reveal traits or leadership styles. Leadership is considered more a style of leading and less of an influencer that impacts the practices or behaviors of followers.

**Table 1.1. Selected literature influencing educational leadership, 1911–1967**

| Year of publication | Author(s) | Title of book | Major themes | Discipline |
|---|---|---|---|---|
| 1911 | F. Taylor | *Principles of Scientific Management* | Efficiency, initiative and incentive, command and control | Business |
| 1925 | M. Weber | *The Theory of Social and Economic Organization* | Legal-bureaucratic, traditional, charismatic | Sociology |
| 1959 | R. E. Dupuy & T. N. Dupuy | *Brave Men and Great Captains* | The Heroic Leader and Trait Theory: Leaders are in control and provide leadership for followers. | U.S. military |
| 1964 | R. R. Blake & J. S. Mouton | *The Managerial Grid* | The grid or quadrant emerges and leads to style: the leader directs and coordinates the work of others. | Military, business |
| 1967 | F. Fiedler | *A Theory of Leadership Effectiveness* | Directing and coordinating the work of the group | Business |

## Transformational Leadership and the Learning Organization, 1978–1990

Table 1.2 covers the 1970s, the 1980s, and the beginning of the 1990s. Political scientist John McGregor Burns (1978) shifts the emphasis of the leader-centric thinking in the late 1970s by introducing the idea of the transformational leader. Burns asserts the idea that a leader should transform the environment and, indirectly, the followers. Thus begins the journey of an adjective preceding the word leadership. Joseph Rost (1993) regards the 1980s as an era with an updated version of the great man/woman or heroic leader. He characterizes this period as "do the leader's wishes" (70).

Complexity and how organizations and individuals need to respond are major themes of the leadership literature in the 1980s and 1990s. Peter Senge establishes a need for the learning organization in the book *Fifth Discipline* (Senge et al. 1994). Donald Schon (1983) introduces the idea of refining the individual's skills and capabilities. Senge sees the complexity in the world that the organization will encounter, and Schon sees the need for individuals to acquire and refine their intrapersonal and interpersonal skill sets. Complexity in the world necessitates that the individual must learn through and reflect upon feedback.

Teaching is described in the era of the 1980s as veridical in nature, delivered mostly in a whole-group configuration. The word *veridical* is based upon the Latin root word for truth. Veridical teaching is the transmission of factual information (truth), whereby learning is a passive activity. For the book *A Place Called School* (1984), John Goodlad and a team of researchers visit sixty-seven schools—150 classrooms—in thirteen states. The team observes

> the teacher explaining/lecturing to the total class, asking direct, factual-type questions or monitoring or observing students; the students "listening" to the teacher or responding to the teacher-initiated interaction. The majority of students at all schooling levels—nearly two-thirds in elementary and three fourths in secondary—work as a total class—less than 10% are found working in small group configurations. (10, 14)

Goodlad notes "remarkably similar" programs and teaching irrespective of local differences. He is disappointed and notes across all schools there is "a flatness" to teaching. He documents teaching practices that were initially established for the industrial age. The job of the teacher is viewed as an interchangeable part that could be readily replaced. Teaching is viewed as

**Table 1.2. Selected literature influencing educational leadership, 1978–1990**

| Year of publication | Author(s) | Title of book | Major themes | Discipline |
|---|---|---|---|---|
| 1978 | J. M. Burns | Leadership | Transformational leader, i.e., leadership is a transactional process with the followership. | Political science |
| 1983 | D. Schon | Reflective Practitioner | Learning-in-action interpersonal and intrapersonal dimensions | Business |
| 1984 | J. Goodlad | A Place Called School | Study of teaching across states concludes a flatness and sameness to teaching with teacher-focused instruction a dominant theme. | Education |
| 1989 | S. Covey | The Seven Habits of Highly Effective People | Principles; values; seek first to understand, then to be understood; and interdependence | Business |
| 1990 | P. Senge | The Fifth Discipline | Learning organization, mental models, team learning, and systems thinking | Business |

a technical skill, whereby transmitting information is the dominant theme of the learning process.

## Adaptive Leadership a Response for Addressing Complexity, 1993–2003

Table 1.3 covers the mid-1990s through the mid-2000s. Margaret Wheatley (1992) introduces chaos and complexity as organizational realities. She forcefully and thoughtfully criticizes the ongoing reliance upon heroic leadership. A new science of leadership needs to emerge if individuals and organizations are to adapt to a complex and chaotic world. Ron Heifetz (1994) produces a framework for understanding organizational complexity and change as a combination of technical problems and adaptive challenges. Adaptive leadership begins with a leader's ability to diagnose a situation and learn from keen observation, a process known as the balcony view.

Few educational researchers had explored the link between school leadership and student learning in a systematic manner until Philip Hallinger and Ronald Heck in 1998. Les Bell, Ray Bolam, and Leela Cubillo, in 2003, explore the relationship between school leadership and student learning by reviewing eight studies. The possibility of a researched knowledge base linking school leadership with student learning starts to emerge.

## The Agile Organization and Adaptive Leadership, 2005–2009

Table 1.4 covers 2005 through 2009. The U.S. military searches for the best methods for preparing military leaders in an age of complexity, and the U.S. Department of Defense establishes the Command and Control Research Center. Simon Atkinson and James Moffat provide a rationale for military leadership to embrace the agile organization (2005) and assert the historical conceptions of command and control are outdated. The formal organization has to work in concert with those in the field by empowering network-centric groups to solve complex problems.

Robert Marzano, Timothy Waters, and Brian McNulty, in *School Leadership That Works: From Research to Results* (2005), perform a meta-analysis and establish a link between twenty-one responsibilities and student academic achievement. For their meta-analysis, the authors refine the twenty-five categories identified by Kathleen Cotton in 2003 in her narrative review of the literature linking principals' responsibilities with student achievement. The meta-analysis by Marzano, Waters, and McNulty is one

**Table 1.3.  Selected literature influencing educational leadership, 1992–2003**

| Year of publication | Author(s) | Title of book | Major themes | Discipline |
|---|---|---|---|---|
| 1992 | M. Wheatley | *Leadership and the New Science: Discovering Order in a Chaotic World* | Order from chaos/complexity, relationships, information as source of change, critique of the heroic leader | Business |
| 1993 | J. Rost | *Leadership for the Twenty-First Century* | A synopsis of the last 75 years of leadership in the postindustrial era | Eclectic |
| 1994 | R. Heifetz | *Leadership without Easy Answers* | Adaptive leadership (technical problems and adaptive challenges) | Business |
| 1998 | P. Hallinger & R. Heck | *Exploring the Principal's Contribution to School Effectiveness: 1980–1995* | Principals have a modest impact on student learning. | Education |
| 2003 | L. Bell, R. Bolam & L. Cubillo | *A Systematic Review of the Impact of School Head Teachers and Principals on Student Outcomes* | Eight studies located for examining leadership and student learning | Education |

**Table 1.4.** Selected literature influencing educational leadership, 2005–2009

| Year of publication | Author(s) | Title of book | Major themes | Discipline |
|---|---|---|---|---|
| 2005 | S. R. Atkinson & J. Moffat | *The Agile Organization: From Informal Networks to Complex Effects and Agility* | Transformation of command and control to network-centric environments, complex adaptive systems, and nonlinear interactions | U.S. military, Department of Defense |
| 2005 | R. Marzano, T. Waters & B. McNulty | *School Leadership That Works: From Research to Results* | Meta-analysis of the link between school leadership and student achievement—70 studies, 60 unpublished theses or conference papers | Education |
| 2006 | T. Wagner et al. | *Change Leadership: A Practical Guide to Transforming Our Schools* | Thinking systematically, reframing, instruction, disciplines to overcome, too many initiatives | Education |
| 2009 | J. Hattie | *Visible Learning: A Synthesis of Over 800 Meta-Analyses Relating to Achievement* | Research literature is rich in what works, "ideas" are ranked by effect size, and teacher expertise is a major theme. | Education |
| 2009 | R. A. Heifetz, A. Grashow & M. Linsky | *The Practice of Adaptive Leadership: Tools and Tactics for Changing Your Organization and the World* | Adaptive challenges and technical problems, trust, experimentation | Business |

of the first substantive studies that linked school leadership with student learning.

John Hattie, in *Visible Learning: A Synthesis of Over 800 Meta-Analyses Relating to Achievement* (2009), clarifies the muddy waters of "what works" by synthesizing more than eight hundred meta-analyses (fifty thousand studies) relating to influences on achievement in school-aged students. Effective teaching practices are considered more complex than the classrooms that were observed by John Goodlad (1984) in the 1970s and 1980s.

Tony Wagner and numerous colleagues, in *Change Leadership: A Practical Guide to Transforming Our Schools* (2006), note that "leaders must understand and bring together the challenges of both organization and individual change to successfully lead improvement processes in schools and district" (193). Many organizational reform efforts focus on either reforming the organizational structure or enhancing the skill set of individuals or groups. Wagner and his colleagues assert that improvement of both the organization and the individual must happen simultaneously.

Ronald Heifetz, Alexander Grashow, and Marty Linsky (2009) further the field's understanding of adaptive leadership. The authors affirm that trust, collaboration, flexibility, and experimentation are capabilities needed by leaders in an era of complexity. Adaptive leadership is a new model of leadership that recognizes the information age needs a more nuanced view of leading than the centralized control established in the industrial age.

## A Home of Our Own Emerges: Leading Linked with Student Learning, 2010–2013

Table 1.5 covers the years 2010 through 2013, and the conversation about linking leadership with student learning takes center stage. Hanna Dumont, David Istance, and Francisco Benavides, in *The Nature of Learning: Using Research to Inspire Practice* (2010), articulate that teaching in the industrial age can be characterized as veridical and predominately instructor-centric. Due to the complexity of learning in the information age, however, now teaching needs to be more adaptive and learner-centric.

Dumont, Istance, and Benavides assert that creating innovative learning environments should be regarded as pedagogies of contingency, or a constantly adaptive endeavor. They also assert that adaptive competence, an ultimate goal of learning, is a combination of mastering content knowledge, applying metacognitive strategies, and the ability of learners to self-regulate and monitor their emotional states.

**Table 1.5. Selected literature influencing educational leadership, 2010–2013**

| Year of publication | Author(s) | Title of book | Major themes | Discipline |
|---|---|---|---|---|
| 2010 | H. Dumont, D. Istance & F. Benavides (Eds.) | The Nature of Learning: Using Research to Inspire Practice | Designing innovative learning environment, integrate an understanding of content, student motivation, emotion, and metacognition | Education |
| 2011 | V. Robinson | Student-Centered Leadership | Based on best evidence synthesis (BES), 27 studies establish the link between leadership and student learning: not leadership style, rather practices and capabilities. | Education |
| 2012 | K. Leithwood & K. Seashore Louis | Linking Leadership to Student Learning | Review and analysis of the link between leadership and student learning, original research both qualitative and quantitative | Education |
| 2013 | L. Cuban | Inside the Black Box of Classroom Practice: Change without Reform in American Education | Historical overview of structural and incremental reforms and policies and the influence on teacher classroom practice | Education |
| 2013 | D. Goleman | Focus: The Hidden Driver of Excellence | Leadership: capturing, directing, and keeping our collective attention | Business |

Two groups of researchers, led by Viviane Robinson and Kenneth Leithwood respectively, establish a solid, research-based foundation for educational leadership at the school level for the first time. The book *Student-Centered Leadership* (2011) by Viviane Robinson is grounded in the best evidence synthesis (BES) of research developed with her colleagues Margie Hohepa and Claire Lloyd and published in 2009. The 290-page BES study is groundbreaking work, and a debt of gratitude is owed to the New Zealand Ministry of Education for supporting this work.

The BES was an investigation of the link between educational leadership and the core business of teaching and learning. Robinson writes that her work was supported by "the shift from leadership style to leadership practices" (3). This is a significant departure from the leader-centric conceptions of leadership that emerged in the early 1900s in the literature. Viviane Robinson asserts, "Leadership styles such as transformational, transactional, democratic or authentic leaderships are abstract concepts that tell us little about the behaviors involved and how to learn them" (3).

The book *Linking Leadership to Student Learning* (2012), by Kenneth Leithwood and Karen Seashore Louis, is based upon investigations from 2004 to 2010 that are well documented by the numerous Learning from Leadership Project reports commissioned by the Wallace Foundation (e.g., Leithwood, Seashore Louis, Anderson, and Wahlstrom 2004). These reports provide a solid research-based foundation for linking school-level research to student learning, and significantly advance understanding of how school-level leadership influences the learning of students, which is the reason schools exist.

Daniel Goleman, in the book *Focus: The Hidden Driver of Excellence* (2013), notes that "leadership itself hinges on effectively capturing and directing the collective attention" (210). The recognition of the complexity in the information age is awash in information that is challenging to sift through and prioritize. The need for an organization to focus will become a primary leadership capability. Andy Hargreaves and Michael Fullan, in *Professional Capital: Transforming Teaching in Every School* (2012), suggest one path to transforming teaching in the information age is recognizing that human, social, and decisional capital must be combined.

Larry Cuban reminds us, in *Inside the Black Box of Classroom Practice: Change without Reform in American Education* (2013), that few school reforms across the past 150 years seek to alter instructional practices on a systemic level, and few make it past the classroom door, or the "black box."

The classroom door is the equivalent to the blood-brain barrier (a collection of high-density cells that restrict certain substances from entering the brain) in medicine. By establishing stringent rules and inflexible structures at the classroom level, formal organizations can inadvertently foster a tendency to reinforce the closed-classroom door barrier.

## Summary of the Five Tables and Twenty-Five Important Books for Leadership and Learning

The numerous theories, philosophies, and conceptions of leadership presented in tables 1.1 to 1.5 contribute to the difficulties in defining educational leadership. Borrowing ideas and terminology from other disciplines has advanced understanding of leadership broadly defined and has also sowed the seeds of confusion for educational leadership.

Understanding the themes identified in the twenty-five cited books sheds light on the question that was asked earlier in the chapter: why is school leadership the way it is? Until recently, those specific skills, practices, and capabilities deployed by school-level leaders that influenced student learning were not researched or well understood. Layered upon the dilemma of clearly defining school-level leadership is the complexity of the information age. At a time when there is a critical need for strengthening leadership in school, there is now a research base that explicitly links student learning with leadership dispositions, capabilities, and practices.

With an eye on education reform, many policies, such as No Child Left Behind (NCLB; 2002), focused on the formal organization and centered our attention on rules, structures, and regulations. Recent efforts with professional development and professional-learning communities focused on developing the skills and capabilities of the individuals within the system. The literature of Atkinson and Moffat (2005) draws our attention to the need for building network-centric groups that are capable of addressing the complexities of the information age.

The agile organization is one that focuses on refining the organizational structure as well as simultaneously enhancing the skill set and capabilities of individuals through network-centric groups that work interdependently. It is through the use of network-centric groups that educators will become equipped to accomplish problem solving within the complex adaptive systems that transcend the "black box" of the classroom in the twenty-first century.

**Table 1.6. Side-by-side comparisons of Robinson's leadership dimensions and Leithwood's core leadership practices**

| Leadership dimensions: effects of leadership on student outcomes, by Viviane Robinson[1] | Meaning of dimension | Four categories of core leadership practices, by Leithwood and Seashore Louis[2] | Practices typically associated with category |
|---|---|---|---|
| Establishing goals and expectations | Includes the setting, communicating, and monitoring of learning goals, standards, and expectations, and the involvement of the staff and others in the process so there is clarity and consensus about goals | Setting directions | Identifying and articulating a shared vision; fostering the acceptance of group goals, communication, and creating high performance expectations |
| Ensuring quality teaching | Direct involvement in the support and evaluation of teaching through regular classroom visits and the provision of formative and summative feedback to teachers. Direct oversight of curriculum through schoolwide coordination across classes and year levels and alignment to school goals | Improving the instructional program | Resource alignment, staffing, providing instructional support, and monitoring school activity |
| Resourcing strategically | Involves aligning resource selection and allocation to priority teaching goals and staff recruitment; how to evaluate and reconfigure existing patterns of resource allocation, not how to acquire additional resources; courage to face emotional reactions | Refining and aligning the school organization | Strengthening district and school cultures, modifying organizational structures, and building collaborative processes |

| Leading teacher learning and development | Leadership that not only promotes but also directly participates with teachers in formal or informal professional learning | Developing people | Offering intellectual stimulation, providing individualized support, providing an appropriate model (informal most powerful), and providing individualized support |
| Ensuring an orderly and safe environment | Protecting time for teaching and learning by reducing external pressures and interruptions and establishing an orderly and supportive environment both inside and outside classrooms | Improving the instructional program | Buffering (protecting the staff from distractions) |

1. V. Robinson (2011), *Student-centered leadership* (San Francisco: Jossey-Bass), 12–16.

2. K. Leithwood and K. Seashore Louis (2012), *Linking leadership to student learning* (San Francisco: Jossey-Bass), 59–61.

## A NEW ERA OF LEADERSHIP WITH STUDENT LEARNING AS THE PERVASIVE FOCUS

This chapter began by distinguishing between *leadership in education* and *educational leadership*. The distinction is necessary to acknowledge the rich leadership history while recognizing that a research base unique to school leadership allows educators to explore how to provide productive, innovative learning environments for both students and adults.

As noted earlier, there are two groups of researchers, led by Viviane Robinson and Kenneth Leithwood, who established a solid research base linking school leadership to student learning. First, the findings of the Robinson and Leithwood research teams on what we describe as "broader-grained" leadership dimensions and leadership practices will be explored and compared. Second, the "finer-grained" *three capabilities* by Robinson and the *four leadership pathways* by Leithwood will be described.

### Leadership Dimensions and Core Leadership Practices: Broader-Grained Work

A more refined set of leadership dimensions or practices specific to school leaders began to emerge in the late 1980s. Elaborated on in table 1.6 are Viviane Robinson's leadership dimensions and Kenneth Leithwood's core leadership practices based on extensive literature reviews of school leadership. The side-by-side comparison of the dimensions and practices identified as the broader-grained work reveals a significant convergence of understanding of school-level leadership.

There are two important overarching contributions by Robinson: (1) the relationship between the dimensions and student learning, and (2) the need to distribute leadership due to the complexity of leading a school. Robinson notes, in *Student-Centered Leadership* (2011), that "the scope of the work is too great and the expertise too broad to reasonably expect a single leader to demonstrate high or even moderate levels of competence in all five dimensions" (15).

Practicing principals will likely agree that the dimension of ensuring an orderly and safe environment is the foundation for the other four dimensions. Interestingly, the dimension of leading teacher learning and development had the highest effect size (0.84) on student outcomes in the meta-analysis performed by the Robinson research team. Principals who learn side by side with teachers model the importance of a growth mindset.

Kenneth Leithwood and Karen Seashore Louis, in the book *Linking Leadership to Student Learning* (2012), identify four categories of core leadership practices, as noted on the right side of table 1.6. The authors state that reviews of empirical research and illustrative studies support the claim that "these practices ought to be an essential part of the repertoire of school leaders" (59). Leithwood and Seashore Louis identify setting direction and exercising influence as core functions that are indispensable to implementing the core leadership practices.

Leithwood and Seashore Louis's four categories of core leadership practices are similar to the five dimensions identified by Robinson and can only be accomplished by distributing leadership at the school level. Leithwood and Robinson both assert that the impact of formal school leadership on student learning is mostly indirect. There is a critical role function for the agile organization—the district-level formal organization—to plan to assist school leaders with the broader-grained work. The agile organization establishes conditions for productive work and understands the limitation of direct influence on student learning.

## The Three Capabilities and Four Pathways: Finer-Grained Leadership Work

Described in table 1.7 are Robinson's three capabilities and Leithwood's four leadership pathways. These capabilities and pathways are the finer-grained work of school-level leadership. Robinson's three capabilities are building relational trust, applying relevant knowledge, and solving complex problems. Leithwood's four leadership pathways are the emotions, rational, organizational, and family. These capabilities and pathways are displayed in a side-by-side manner to suggest they contain similar attributes.

It is essential to understand that Robinson and Leithwood suggest that leadership is about influencing others through the use of three capabilities and four pathways. Leithwood and Robinson intentionally use the word *leadership* and not *leader* to broadly define the use of capabilities and pathways. Leadership is not limited to a person with positional power because the impact of the work of a principal on student learning is indirect.

These insights are a significant departure from the leader-centric role of a heroic leader and control of information and decision making through a hierarchal bureaucracy. New routines and patterns of working with colleagues and an expanded set of skills for working with students will require engaging teachers in the challenging work. School leaders will need to discover and develop approaches to influence others and focus the school

**Table 1.7. Side-by-side comparisons of Robinson's capabilities and Leithwood's leadership pathways**

| Robinson's three capabilities (finer-grained knowledge, skills, and dispositions)[1] | Attributes | Three of Leithwood's four* leadership pathways[2] | Attributes |
|---|---|---|---|
| Building relational trust | Develop the trust that is essential for doing the hard work of improving teaching and learning (can't achieve much on your own); engage others in the work that delivers for learners; show respect (valuing the ideas of others), trustworthiness, competence, and integrity. | Emotions path (emotions direct cognition) | Commitment, networking among the staff, teacher efficacy, and collective efficacy (leads to persistence through trust and positive morale) |
| Applying relevant knowledge | Deepen teacher knowledge; develop expertise to do the work, using knowledge about effective teaching, teacher learning, and school organization to make high-quality administrative decisions. | Rational path | Quality of instruction, standards and curriculum (*technical core* for student learning); establishing high expectations, shared goals about academic achievement, orderly environment, and problem-solving capabilities |
| Solving complex problems | All about context specific to each school; take many conditions into account for making decisions; discern challenges and craft solutions that adequately address them. | Organizational path | School infrastructure, professional networks, structures to support collaboration, instructional time, complexity of teachers' workload, opportunities for teachers' growth, time devoted to instruction |

*Family path not included.

1. V. Robinson (2011). *Student-centered leadership* (San Francisco: Jossey-Bass), 22–38.

2. K. Leithwood, K. Anderson, M. Blair, and T. Strauss (2009). School leaders' influences on student learning: The four paths, in T. Bush, L. Bell, and D. Middlewood (Eds.), *The principles of educational leadership and management* (London: Sage).

on improving student learning through applying relevant knowledge about teaching and learning.

In the recent era of NCLB accountability, building relational trust and the emotions path were superseded by solely focusing on the technical aspects of schooling. The technical aspects of schooling are noted in Leithwood's rational and organizational paths, as well as Robinson's capability of applying relevant knowledge. The technical aspects of schooling are extraordinarily important and should be key areas of focus for school-level leaders. However, teaching and learning cannot be improved without understanding the importance of building relational trust, as noted by Robinson, and nurturing collective efficacy, as observed by Leithwood.

Learning as a pervasive focus of a school places educational leadership apart from the previous models described as leadership in education earlier in this chapter. Dumont, Istance, and Benavides note: "The emotional and cognitive dimensions of learning are inextricably intertwined" (2010, 15) in the process of teaching students, as well as for leading adults in schools. Creating innovative learning environments in schools that take into account the interplay of emotion, motivation, and cognition is not well served by imposing numerous private-sector business principles.

## SUMMARY

The literature reviewed in this chapter is foundational for a contemporary understanding of leadership. Since the early 1900s, leadership in education was based upon theories by authors representing many disciplines other than education. The question was asked earlier in the chapter, why is it so hard to change leadership structure? One possible answer is the dominant and persistent leader-centric themes in the literature that focus on the leader's abilities, characteristics, and styles.

Recently, Robinson and Leithwood, with their respective colleagues, have provided a much deeper understanding of the link between school leadership and student learning. An effective formal leader is still extremely important—a leader with a mental model of educational leadership that suggests leadership is about distributing the dispositions, capabilities, and practices that influence student learning.

An unavoidable reality for student learning in the information age will be exposure to greater levels of cognitive complexity in content domains. Therefore, an additional understanding for educational leadership, or a home of our own, will be the need to design innovative learning environments for increased student and adult learning. Learners engaging in greater levels of cognitive complexity will also need to self-regulate both their emotions and motivations. In recent school reform efforts where improvement was viewed as simply a technical issue, the roles of emotion and motivation were viewed as not relevant.

The difficult work of constantly applying relevant knowledge to improve the technical core of instruction will create a need for continuous learning by all members of the educational organization. The challenge of solving complex problems cannot be accomplished by one person in the positional role of principal. Building relational trust and the emotions path, as described by Robinson and Leithwood (see table 1.7), will be preconditions that leaders will need to constantly monitor for the work of applying relevant knowledge and solving complex problems.

There is a need to rethink the school leader's role with a transition away from an overemphasis on the qualities of the leader to a broader view of leadership as developing the facility to influence thinking and distribute expertise throughout a complex school organization. The information age requires continuous ongoing learning by adults to solve complex problems and address adaptive challenges in a trusting and engaged community. School leaders will need to be equipped to successfully lead in this complex environment.

This book identifies five dispositions of leadership that are defined by the thinking, capabilities, and practices for distributing leadership within a school community. These five dispositions are described in more detail in chapters 4 through 8. Educational leadership, a home of our own, is incomplete until the foundation is fortified with these five dispositions of leadership.

As noted earlier in this chapter, the work of improving schools requires that change happen within the organization and individuals simultaneously. The next chapter will describe the historical formal organization and examine what is needed in an agile organization for leading schools in the information age.

## QUESTIONS TO ENGAGE YOUR THINKING AND DISCUSSION WITH COLLEAGUES

1. What contrasts can you draw between the heroic leader and the findings of Robinson's capabilities and Leithwood's pathways?

2. As you reflect on this chapter, what major insights linger with you as you make decisions about your own leadership related to student learning?

## REFERENCES

Alhstrom, S. (2004). *A religious history of the American people*. New Haven, CT: Yale University Press.

Atkinson, S. R., and Moffat, J. (2005). *The agile organization: From informal networks to complex effects and agility*. Information Age Transformation Series. Washington, DC: DOD Command and Control Research Program. Available at http://www.dodccrp.org/files/Atkinson_Agile.pdf.

Bell, L., Bolam, R., and Cubillo L. (2003). *A systematic review of the impact of school head teachers and principals on student outcomes*. London: EPPI-Centre, Social Science Research Unit, Institute of Education.

Burns, J. M. (1978). *Leadership*. New York: Harper.

Cotton, K. (2003). *Principals and student achievement: What the research says*. Alexandria, VA: Association for Supervision and Curriculum Development.

Cuban, L. (2013). *Inside the black box of classroom practice: Change without reform in American education*. Cambridge, MA: Harvard Education Press.

Dumont, H., Istance, D., and Benavides, F. (Eds.) (2010). *The nature of learning: Using research to inspire practice*. Paris: Organisation for Economic Co-operation and Development, Innovative Learning Environments Project.

Goleman, D. (2013). *Focus: The hidden driver of excellence*. New York: Harper-Collins.

Goodlad, J. (1984). *A place called school: Prospects for the future*. New York: McGraw-Hill.

Hallinger, P., and Heck, R. (1998). Exploring the principal's contribution to school effectiveness: 1980–1995. *School Effectiveness and School Improvement, 9*(2), 157–191.

Hargreaves, A., and Fullan, M. (2012). *Professional capital: Transforming teaching in every school*. New York: Teachers College Press.

Hattie, J. (2009). *Visible learning: A synthesis of over 800 meta-analyses relating to achievement*. New York: Routledge.

Heifetz, R. (1994). *Leadership without easy answers*. Cambridge, MA: Belknap Press of Harvard University Press.

Heifetz, R. A., Grashow, A., and Linsky, M. (2009). *The practice of adaptive leadership: Tools and tactics for changing your organization and the world*. Boston: Harvard Business Press.

Leithwood, K., Anderson, K., Blair, M., and Strauss, T. (2009). School leaders' influences on student learning: The four paths. In T. Bush, L. Bell, and D. Middlewood (Eds.), *The principles of educational leadership and management*. London: Sage.

Leithwood, K., and Seashore Louis, K. (2012). *Linking leadership to student learning*. San Francisco: Jossey-Bass.

Leithwood, K., Seashore Louis, K. S., Anderson, S., and Wahlstrom, K. (2004). *How leadership influences student learning*. New York: Wallace Foundation.

Marzano, R., Waters, T., and McNulty, B. (2005). *School leadership that works: From research to results*. Alexandria, VA: Association for Supervision and Curriculum Development.

No Child Left Behind Act of 2001, Pub. L. No. 107–110, 115, Stat. 1425 (2002).

Robinson, V. (2011). *Student-centered leadership*. San Francisco: Jossey-Bass.

Robinson, V., Hohepa, M., and Lloyd, C. (2009). *School leadership and student outcomes: Identifying what works and why (BES)*. Wellington: New Zealand Ministry of Education.

Rost, J. (1993). *Leadership for the twenty-first century*. Westport, CT: Praeger.

Schon, D. (1983). *The reflective practitioner: How professionals think in action*. New York: Basic.

Senge, P., Roberts, C., Ross, R., Smith, B., and Kleiner, A. (1994). *The fifth discipline fieldbook: Strategies and tools for building a learning organization*. New York: Doubleday.

Taylor, F. (1911). *Principles of scientific management*. New York: Harper and Brothers.

Tyack, D., and Hansot, E. (1982). *Managers of virtue: Public school leadership in America, 1820–1980*. New York: HarperCollins.

Wagner, T., Kegan, R., Lahey, L., Lemons, R. W., Garnier, J., Helsing, D., Rasmussen, H. T., et al. (2006). *Change leadership: A practical guide to transforming our schools*. San Francisco: Jossey-Bass.

Weber, M. (1925). *The theory of social and economic organization*. (A. M. Henderson and T. Parsons, Trans.). New York: Free Press.

Wheatley, M. (1992). *Leadership and the new science: Discovering order in a chaotic world*. San Francisco: Berrett-Koehler.

# 2

# HOW DOES AN AGILE ORGANIZATION SUPPORT CONTEMPORARY SCHOOL LEADERSHIP?

In Industrial Age management, we have, as a given, low agility of the management system due to its unlinked and hierarchical nature.

—Simon Atkinson and James Moffat,
*The Agile Organization* (2005, 127)

**T**he assertion was made at the beginning of this book that effective school leadership in the information age needs to be informed by research on the relationship between school leadership and student learning, described in chapter 1. The assertion was also made that this foundational understanding of the relationship between leadership and student learning needed to be accompanied by a foundational understanding of organizational structures that provide the needed flexibility to adapt to, and thrive in, today's complex learning environments.

The contemporary formal organization in the United States, with its reliance on bureaucratic procedures and structures due to legislative and legal control of public education, lacks the agility needed to effectively respond to complex problems. Andreas Schleicher (2011) makes the observation that the United States will need to make major changes to the educational system to match the flexibility used currently in the highest-performing countries. He notes the top-down initiatives and reforms that do not address the instructional core of teaching are areas the highest-performing countries identified as problematic.

The formal organization, in this case, the school system, is rarely considered a vital partner in efforts to change either the structure and routines of individual schools or the delivery of instruction at the classroom level. Major themes in the literature about schooling focus on improving school-level performance of selected schools or developing skills by altering practices of individuals. The school system is rarely the focus of change efforts, and omitting it from consideration for planned innovations has had the consequence that reforms are idiosyncratic and not systematic.

Therefore, two key ideas will be explored in this chapter. First, individual, group, and organizational change efforts need to be interconnected. Second, the formal organization needs refinement in order to create the conditions for addressing complex problems and solving adaptive challenges. Tony Wagner and colleagues (2006) note that "leaders must understand and bring together the challenges of both organizational and individual change to successfully lead improvement processes in schools and districts" (193).

We further suggest that organizational and individual changes are interconnected and need to be addressed simultaneously. Many educational reforms address isolated skills and practices implemented at the school or classroom level and are independent of meaningful influence by district-level leadership. Improving the skill sets of principals without simultaneously changing the role of the formal organization has not been sustainable or impactful.

It seems clear that the formal organization needs to make adjustments and refine certain organizational structures in order to become an agile organization that supports contemporary school leadership. This chapter will provide an overview of the formal organization, including a description of its limitations. In addition, this chapter will explore why agile organizations and network-centric groups—small collaborative structures—are needed to adapt to the unique and unpredictable learning environments of our educational system in order to address adaptive challenges and engage in complex problem solving.

## THE FORMAL ORGANIZATION: AN OVERVIEW

The formal organization, with command-and-control management structures, remains pervasive in many public institutions and private companies. Figure 2.1 depicts the formal organization. Critiques of command-and-control, formal, and bureaucratic organizations are often polemics about what is wrong with "the system" and why it is dysfunctional. Manual labor required routine, predictable, and simple tasks that did not require complex thinking. It was thought that efficient workers needed a simple and clearly defined hierarchy so they could create and manufacture products on a mass scale.

An industrial age command-and-control structure is defined as having low agility as a system and lacking the ability to respond quickly to its external environment. Chapter 1 noted Fredrick Taylor's (1911) principles of efficiency and Max Weber's (1925) descriptions of bureaucracy and expertise that formed important elements of today's formal organization. These pillars of the formal organization, with a reliance on command-and-control structures, have been used in public education since the 1920s.

Simon Atkinson and James Moffat (2005) created figure 2.1 as a representation of how the low agility of the formal organization resulted from the fact that it was created to organize and control individuals and information in the industrial age. This model of the formal organization is well established in school systems.

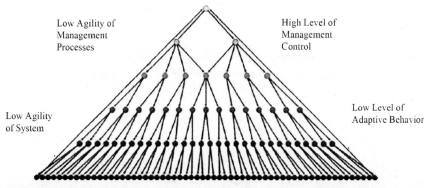

**Figure 2.1. Industrial age command and control.** *Adapted from Atkinson and Moffet (2005, 156).*

Textbox 2.1 notes the system-centric attributes of the formal organization developed to address the need of organizations in the industrial age to accomplish routine manual tasks efficiently. The system was designed to be rule based, predictable, bureaucratic, and compliant, with information controlled by a few at the top of the hierarchy. Procedures are to be followed based on the assumption that uniformity of exposure will lead to uniformity of outcome. Learning is therefore prescriptive, minimizing the variables that impact quality control.

**Textbox 2.1. The formal organization:
system-centric attributes**

Rule based
Linear system and inflexible
Hierarchical and predictable
Bureaucratic and compliant
Information controlled
Predetermined procedures
Synchronous patterns of behavior expected
Learning as a prescriptive activity
Leaders direct subordinates

The major role of a leader in this formal organization is to direct subordinates to follow the procedures and to carefully monitor their behavior for compliance. The formal organization was constructed perfectly for repetitive high-volume work where problem-solving skills were only needed on a limited basis.

## FORMAL ORGANIZATION: ROUTINE ANALYTICAL AND ROUTINE COGNITIVE PROBLEM SOLVING

The design of the formal organization was originally developed in the industrial age to address routine cognitive and routine analytical tasks, as noted in figure 2.2. Certainly, some challenges faced by contemporary organizations could be solved with routine analytical and cognitive processes. Many organizations promote the use of routine analytical and cognitive thinking due to policies and procedures that are applied when problems and challenges are encountered. The assumption, embedded firmly in organizations since the industrial age, is that solving problems follows a linear progression with predictable steps leading to resolution.

However, the routine analytical and routine cognitive problem solving inherent in the system-centric formal organization was not designed to respond to complex problems or address adaptive challenges encountered by groups or individuals. (Adaptive challenges are significant changes and create a temporary loss of competence and identity for individuals within an organization.) The attributes of a formal organizational system, as noted in

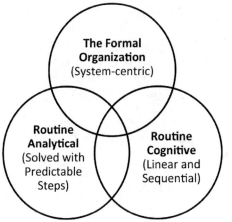

**Figure 2.2. The formal organization: routine problem solving**

textbox 2.1, cannot meaningfully create an environment to unbraid and disentangle complex ideas, concepts, and problems for individuals or groups.

## AGILE ORGANIZATIONS: ADAPTING THE FORMAL ORGANIZATION TO MEET TWENTY-FIRST-CENTURY NEEDS

Business, medicine, education, and the U.S. military are encountering an era in the information age whereby traditional, formal, and command-and-control models are in need of revision. Organizations need new models and new thinking in the face of complexity. However, it is unrealistic, naïve, and ill advised to think that the traditional formal organizations of school systems and schools should or could be replaced.

What is realistic is to adapt the current formal organization in order to support individual and group responses to complex problems and adaptive challenges. Solutions for addressing complexity will ultimately lie in gleaning the best from traditional formal organizational thinking while developing models that will accommodate and respond to an era of extraordinary complexity.

One model that will allow school systems and schools to effectively address the challenges of the information age is an adaptation of the formal organization in order to create a more agile organization. An agile organization is capable of establishing network-centric collaborative groups to intelligently respond to complexity. Figure 2.3 depicts an agile organization with

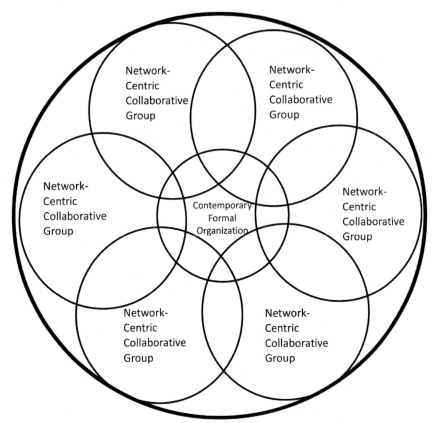

**Figure 2.3. The agile organization: contemporary formal organization with network-centric groups**

the contemporary formal organization at the center creating the conditions necessary to accomplish work across network-centric collaborative groups.

The network-centric collaborative groups at the district, school, and classroom levels (discussed in more detail later in the chapter) are designed to have a more streamlined and effective focus, structure, and set of processes than are traditionally put in place by a formal organization. Network-centric collaborative groups within an agile organization allow schools to effectively address adaptive challenges facing teachers, principals, and school districts in the information age.

This adaptation allows schools to maintain some of their traditional functions while also empowering collaborative decision making and enabling school systems and schools to respond in the environment where challenges are encountered. This model allows formal organizations to adapt the attributes of an agile organization, creating conditions for solving complex problems and addressing adaptive challenges.

An agile organization empowers collaborative decision making and has the capability to respond to challenges in the environment. As noted in textbox 2.2, network-centric collaborative groups within the agile organization are trust based, flexible, adaptive, information enabled, and bounded by collaborative norms of behavior. Learning is a contingency activity based upon the feedback from learners. Therefore, teachers are encouraged to be flexible, and asynchronous patterns of instructional behavior are accepted. An organization needs to be as agile as possible so groups and individuals within the organization can adapt to their environment.

### Textbox 2.2. The agile organization: network-centric group attributes

Trust based
Complex system and flexible
Self-directed and adaptive
Bounded and interactive
Information enabled
Collaborative sensemaking
Asynchronous patterns of behavior acknowledged and accepted
Learning as a contingent activity
Leaders as activators for colleagues

There is a relationship between organizational agility and group or individual adaptability. High agility and high adaptability create the conditions to be responsive to an environment, while low agility and low adaptability are less flexible and less responsive to an environment. The simultaneous work of organizational and individual change is where the idea of the agile organization becomes invaluable in the information age.

The agile organization is equipped to empower individuals or groups to respond to changes, accepting there will be a degree of variability in decision making in order to respond to complex problems. Complexity and complex problems are a common theme in the information age, with examples from natural systems and in humanly constructed social systems.

Leadership capabilities and practices are shared, and leaders activate the expertise and thinking of colleagues.

## AGILE ORGANIZATIONS: NONROUTINE ANALYTICAL AND INTERACTIVE PROBLEM SOLVING

Frank Levy and Richard Murnane (2004), through careful analysis, identified that the tasks carried out by the American workforce from 1969 to 1998 indicate a steady decline of routine manual and cognitive tasks and an increase in expert thinking (nonroutine analytical) and complex communication (nonroutine interactive). The social and work environments have changed significantly and require different sets of capabilities and skills.

Expert thinking is the ability to solve new or novel problems that cannot be solved by the simple application of rules. *Complex communication* is the ability to both transmit information and convey accurately an interpretation to others from multiple sources of data. Figure 2.4 represents the thinking and communication that can be encouraged to address complex topics and problems by network-centric collaborative groups.

Leading schools and teaching children and young adults is rarely simple, often unpredictable, and frequently requires complex problem solving.

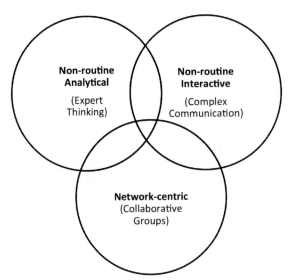

**Figure 2.4. Network-centric groups' complex problem solving**

Charlotte Danielson notes that "more recent research has confirmed that teaching is also cognitively demanding; a teacher makes hundreds of non-trivial decisions daily" (2007, 2). The implementation of new standards changes both the content and the strategies used by teachers.

Additionally, the student population has become more diverse, with increasing numbers of children and young adults with learning challenges and also increasing numbers of students with a first language other than English. Thus, the hundreds of decisions a teacher will make in a day are influenced by new content, new delivery methods, and students with diverse learning and emotional needs.

The observation by Levy and Murnane (2004) of the need for expert thinking and complex communication, and the statement by Danielson about the number of cognitively demanding decisions made by a teacher each day, suggest the need for an agile organization. To be effective, this agile organization must rely on network-centric collaborative groups to influence and support changes needed in schools and classrooms.

## ASSERTING FOCUS AMIDST COMPLEXITY: A CHALLENGE IN THE INFORMATION AGE

A major challenge for the formal organization in the information age is distilling, clarifying, and focusing the attention of all members of the organization. A significant role of district-level leadership is to provide clear focus and direction for all members of the school system. Nancy Dixon (1994) made the important contribution that a connection or alignment in the individual, group, and organizational goals must be made. Therefore, focus is provided by communicating goals, allocating resources, and providing support so all members of the organization can excel at their work.

Conflicting and unfocused messages, too many goals and expectations, and lack of support are often cited as major hurdles in many school systems. Wagner and his colleagues (2006) recognize that the demands of public accountability and responsiveness can create competing priorities that distract and dilute the focus of school leaders. They state, "Simply put, the individual teacher, school, or district with ten priorities has none" (66).

Talented district-level leaders recognize the need to provide focus that influences and inspires across the entire organization. Alan Siegel and Irene Etzkorn (2011) suggest that to address complexity, an idea or concept should be simplified by distilling and clarifying. John Maeda (2000) asserts that thoughtful reduction is the best means to achieve simplicity. A concise and precise message about the focus and direction of a school system is a necessary and significant task for school district leaders.

Distilling, clarifying, or reducing complex ideas in order to achieve simplicity takes time and would be impossible to do with only a formal organizational structure in place. Daniel Goleman (2013) made the powerful assertion that "leadership itself hinges on effectively capturing and directing the collective attention" (210). It is far easier to describe the goals or the focus of an organization than to actually provide meaningful opportunities for groups or individuals to make sense of them, given their respective context and circumstances.

The successful organization in the information age will need to capitalize on the helpful attributes of the formal organization by setting overall direction and providing the resources of time and money, clarity of purpose, and focus. However, simply communicating a message from the leaders of a formal organization to groups and individuals will not be sufficient for maintaining clarity and focus.

The implications of a message that focuses an organization will undoubtedly create adaptive challenges—those challenges that require new beliefs and behaviors in order to find solutions. In order to activate the best in all members of the organization a different structure is needed to facilitate making sense of the direction of an organization for groups and individuals. The organizational structure for addressing the changes needed in education will not be accomplished by building a bigger and better industrial age formal organization with an enhanced command-and-control structure.

Network-centric collaborative groups are designed to interact face-to-face and through web-based platforms. This structure is information enabled, offers flexibility, and promotes asynchronous patterns of behavior by group members in order to respond to problems and challenges. The idea of colleagues being "networked" through technologies to address challenges and complex problems is a structure commonly utilized in business and information technology. Two examples of network-centric collaborative groups are high-performing teams of principals established by district leadership and leadership teams created by principals at the school level.

The agile organization needs to provide two important things for schools and school-level leaders. First, district-level leadership needs to assert the authoritative role of providing clarity of purpose, resources, and focus so school-level leaders can take action. Second, district-level leadership needs to create collaborative groups across the entire organization that will address complex problems and adaptive challenges.

## AGILITY: IDENTIFYING THE TYPE OF PROBLEM OR CHALLENGE

The district leaders responsible for setting the direction of the formal organization demonstrate agility when they develop the capability of identifying the type of change needed in front of them, the thinking best suited to address the change, and where decision-making responsibility should reside. Frequently, formal organization leaders in education adjust the structure of the organization by flattening the hierarchy, implementing site-based management practices, adopting private-sector management principles, creating learning organizations, or forming professional-learning communities.

Educators need to rethink how problems and challenges are thought about in order to clarify understanding of the choices available for moving forward. Responsiveness to an emerging issue and addressing the challenges encountered requires an understanding of the intended cognitive processes envisioned for an agile organization.

### Technical Problems, Adaptive Challenges, and Polarity Management

Agility is the ability to think quickly with intellectual acuity when confronted with challenges, problems, or dilemmas. The first step in exhibiting agility as an organization is identifying and having common terminology for describing the type of problem or challenge that is presented. Three important ideas that assist leaders in thinking about a difficulty or dilemma are technical problems, adaptive challenges, and polarities.

Sharon Daloz Parks (2005) describes a common lack of understanding of the difference between technical problems and adaptive challenges. Daloz Parks notes that

> *technical problems* (even though they may be complex) can be solved with knowledge and procedures already in hand. In contrast, *adaptive challenges* require new learning, innovation, and new patterns of behavior. In this view, leadership is the activity of mobilizing people to address adaptive challenges—those challenges that cannot be resolved by expert knowledge and routine management alone. (10)

The distinction between a technical problem and an adaptive challenge is incredibly important because, as Ronald Heifetz, Alexander Grashow, and Marty Linsky (2009) state, "the most common cause of failure in leadership is produced by treating adaptive challenges as if they were technical problems" (19). Leaders in an agile organization recognize and address both technical problems and adaptive challenges.

Technical problems are often addressed by establishing an action plan and utilizing knowledge and expertise already within the system. Formal organizations, if managed and led well, are equipped to address technical problems on a large scale. When leaders fail to address technical problems, the staff loses confidence that details have been well thought out prior to implementing a program or idea.

Adaptive challenges require new beliefs and behaviors whereby individuals often experience a temporary loss of confidence and identity. An appreciation of both technical problems and adaptive challenges is needed in the era of accountability in public education where implementing new approaches and programs is expected.

District-level leaders especially need an understanding about the nature of adaptive challenges and the potential impact they can have on principals and teachers. Mischaracterizing an adaptive challenge as a simple technical problem can radically influence the potential success of implementing new approaches and programs in schools. An understanding of the definitions of *complicated* and *complex* provides an additional lens for identifying technical problems and adaptive challenges.

Technical problems can be complicated. It is complicated to design and build a jumbo jet. Engineers can design and develop blueprints and create step-by-step algorithms that include many systems that will interact. Building the jumbo jet is highly technical and difficult but usually predictable. Adaptive challenges, and educating children, are complex. Many players interact in unpredictable ways, and there are scores of moving parts. The independent nature of all the players makes identifying a single controlling entity very difficult. An ever-changing landscape of people, policies, and societal expectations requires continual adaptations.

Barry Johnson (2014) introduces the idea of polarities in organizations and in daily lives of individuals. A polarity is an unavoidable issue that defies resolution. Some problems that are encountered cannot be resolved. However, they can be managed. Johnson introduced the concept of polarity management. Many complex problems that are encountered in an agile organization cannot be addressed with either/or thinking.

The industrial age formal organization thinking typically uses routine cognitive and problem-solving strategies that promote either/or thinking. Polarities that are encountered are best viewed by both/and thinking. Two sets of polarities that are frequently encountered in education are (1) the desire for individual autonomy and the need for team collaboration, and (2) coherence and coordination of programs across the system and empowerment and flexibility at the school-site level.

Polarity management is an ongoing process that emphasizes the positive nature of each concept while recognizing the limitation of overemphasizing either pole of the polarity. For example, coherence is needed in a school system implementing programs for all students, and flexibility is also needed to address individual learning needs. Managing this polarity would require a well-honed process and the skillful use of discussion and dialogue by those leading the system-wide implementation.

Table 2.1 lists the characteristics of technical problems, adaptive challenges, and polarities, as well as whether an issue is predictable, routine, complicated, complex, avoidable, or solvable. Leaders in an agile organization recognize and assume the responsibility for identifying and addressing technical problems, adaptive challenges, and polarities.

**Table 2.1. Identifying technical problems, adaptive challenges, and polarities**

| Technical problems | Adaptive challenges | Polarities |
|---|---|---|
| Routine | Nonroutine | Nonroutine |
| Predictable | Not predictable | Unavoidable |
| Complicated | Complex | Unsolvable |

For example, school districts, principals, and teachers, tend to encounter technical problems when new systems are introduced for utilizing student performance data to organize instruction around specific student needs. Technical problems include: access to computers to enter student data, understanding the metrics for analyzing data, creating flexible student groupings, and professional learning opportunities for teachers. District-level leaders in an agile organization understand it is their responsibility to address technical problems throughout the entire system.

Adaptive challenges emerge when new or innovative instructional strategies and flexible grouping practices are planned and implemented based upon the use of student performance data. Teachers and principals will need to discontinue practices that are not particularly effective, accommodate familiar instructional strategies into an existing repertoire, and incorporate unfamiliar techniques into a skill set. Adaptive challenges require new learning and new patterns of behavior, and can often lead to conflict that needs to be addressed with a calm and professional demeanor.

The information age, with complex problems and adaptive challenges that are not predictable, creates a misalignment that the formal organization designed for the industrial age cannot directly address. A different conception of the role of the formal organization is needed. Network-centric collaborative groups are designed to address adaptive challenges and are empowered by an agile organization.

## NETWORK-CENTRIC COLLABORATIVE GROUPS, AGILITY, AND DECISION MAKING

Developing a network-centric collaborative culture is a concrete step toward moving from the direct role of administrative accountability and control to an organization that assumes the indirect role of creating conditions intentionally designed by an agile organization. The role of the agile organization is to

- minimize distraction;
- reduce unnecessary tasks; and
- develop the focus, structures, and processes for collaborative groups.

The direct influence of the formal organization on creating the conditions for groups and individuals has a powerful indirect influence on the ability of networked groups to address complex problems and adaptive challenges. District-level leaders need to realize and acknowledge that network-centric collaborative groups provide the structure and processes for building relational trust and engaging in collaborative sensemaking in order to solve problems and share expertise.

The formal organization needs to adopt the facilitative and activator role that supports network-centric collaborative groups at the district, school, and classroom levels. Solving complex problems at the school or classroom level is simply out of the reach of the formal organization's direct influence. Asserting excessive bureaucratic control tends to stifle creativity, discourage experimentation, and limit decision making.

Network-centric collaborative groups are designed to have a more streamlined and effective focus, structure, and set of processes than are traditionally put in place by a formal organization. It is unlikely that complex problems or adaptive challenges can be adequately addressed unless groups are empowered and encouraged to meet the problems and challenges directly.

Anthony Bryk (2015) observes that the evidence-based practice movement relies heavily upon a formal process of clinical trials and is slow, expensive, and unlikely to be the primary source for improving schools. He advocates establishing networked improvement communities (NIC) to address "two issues—system complexity and the wide variability of performance is key to an effort aimed at systematically improving the productivity of our educational institutions" (469). Network-centric collaborative groups are established to

- address complexity within the system;
- increase and strengthen interdependence as a norm for professional interaction; and
- disseminate expertise and practical information that is foundational for improvement.

Interestingly, many of the policy and school reform prescriptions work through the traditional formal organization with the tools of compliance, accountability, and consequence. The assumption is that solutions to problems can be addressed by applying routine and familiar structures for solving technical problems. A school district cannot simply ignore the increasing demands brought about by statutes and policies at the local, state, and federal level.

However, district leaders can buffer and simplify a message and change the culture of leadership by changing structures, routines, and processes. This is a risky undertaking and can lead to a misalignment between the new expectations and the capabilities of groups and individuals to respond effectively without investing in building capacity and resourcefulness of school-level leaders.

Changing routines and processes is at the core of changing the culture of an organization. Two types of network-centric collaborative groups at the local level that can change routines and transmit insights into solving problems are high-performing teams of principals established by district leadership and leadership teams created by principals at the school level.

## HIGH-PERFORMING PRINCIPAL TEAMS AND SCHOOL-BASED LEADERSHIP TEAMS

The major purposes for creating and supporting high-performing teams of principals are to model, teach, and practice how to function as a network-centric collaborative group. Principals grouped into trios or triads develop and fine-tune how to implement the organizational goals in their particular setting. For instance, a school system might want to improve literacy instruction and student performance in kindergarten through grade 12. Such an initiative will have different implementation strategies at certain grade levels and also need to be interconnected for coherence throughout the system.

The high-performing teams are supported through the five dispositions of leadership that will be described in the remaining chapters of this book—the capabilities and practices that provide practical resources. High-performing teams of principals engage in work that is meaningful and impacts them directly. These school-level leadership teams are designed to support distributing leadership throughout the school.

The leadership team usually comprises members that represent various roles and responsibilities across the school. While task allocation and completion may be a portion of the work of the team, a more prominent role of the leadership team is to assist with fostering capabilities and practices across the school that will support improved student learning. A school-based leadership team serves as a catalyst for establishing and implementing routines and processes that enhance collaboration and complex problem solving on behalf of students' growth.

## SUMMARY

It is sobering to think that headmasters and principals across the world feel ill equipped to lead schools in designing instructional practices that are more aligned with the skills necessary for success in the information age. Regarding the challenges facing school leaders across all the countries participating in the Program for International Student Assessment (PISA), Schleicher (2012) notes,

> Despite the availability of training, school leaders across the Organisation for Economic Co-operation and Development (OECD) countries have often reported that they felt they had not been adequately trained to assume their posts. Although most candidates for school-leadership positions have a teaching background, they are not necessarily competent in pedagogical innovation. (26)

An agile organization must accept the challenge of assisting principals to become brilliant leaders equipped to face the challenges of the information age.

An agile organization creates the conditions so principals can implement new content knowledge for designing innovative learning environments, processes, and routines that support teachers. The role of district-level leadership must change to truly maximize human capital and build the capacity of school-level leaders by forming high-performing teams.

Consideration should be given to structuring ongoing opportunities for aiding principals in developing their resourcefulness to lead when faced with technical problems, adaptive challenges, and polarities. A new model must take into account the adult learning networks in schools that intentionally design a culture of job-embedded learning. Many changes facing school leaders are complex challenges that are not easily solved. Schools need to invest in the capacity of principals by organizing job-embedded learning opportunities that model dispositions of leadership and encourage thoughtful, intentionally designed change.

District-level leaders can advance a student learning agenda by developing high-performing teams to address adaptive challenges. Issuing directives, implementing mandates, and clarifying roles are all part of the bureaucratic life of school organizations. However, relying solely on the historical bureaucratic processes will not resolve the challenges faced by those responsible for making change happen at the school level.

In the past, there have been calls for flattening the hierarchy, implementing site-based management practices, adopting private-sector management principles, creating learning organizations, leading not managing, defining autonomy, and forming professional-learning communities. Many of the prescriptions were not accompanied by system-wide routines or processes that could assist school leaders during implementation.

Thoughtful consideration must be given to constructing and influencing the current work environment of school-level leaders. High-performing teams of principals focused on implementing the many changes they face can successfully lead. The five dispositions of leadership, described in chapters 3 through 8, provide the thinking, capabilities, and practices needed for leading in the information age.

## QUESTIONS TO ENGAGE YOUR THINKING AND DISCUSSION WITH COLLEAGUES

1. How might you describe the attributes of the agile organization to a colleague?

2. How might you apply the attributes of network-centric groups in your collaborative-type meetings?

## REFERENCES

Atkinson, S. R., and Moffat, J. (2005). *The agile organization: From informal networks to complex effects and agility.* Information Age Transformation Series. Washington, DC: DOD Command and Control Research Program. Available at http://www.dodccrp.org/files/Atkinson_Agile.pdf.

Bryk, A. (2015, December). Accelerating how we learn to improve. *Educational Researcher, 44*(89), 467–477.

Daloz Parks, S. (2005). *Leadership can be taught: A bold approach for a complex world.* Boston: Harvard Business School Press.

Danielson, C. (2007). *Enhancing professional practice: A framework for teaching.* Alexandria, VA: Association for Supervision and Curriculum Development.

Dixon, N. (1994). *The organizational learning cycle: How we can learn collectively.* London: McGraw-Hill.

Goleman, D. (2013). *Focus: The hidden driver of excellence.* New York: Harper-Collins.

Heifetz, R. A., Grashow, A., and Linsky, M. (2009). *The practice of adaptive leadership: Tools and tactics for changing your organization and the world.* Boston: Harvard Business Press.

Johnson, B. (2014). *Polarity management: Identifying and managing unsolvable problems.* Amherst, MA: HRD Press.

Levy, F., and Murnane, R. (2004). *The new division of labor: How computers are creating the next job market.* Princeton, NJ: Princeton University Press.

Maeda, J. (2000). *The laws of simplicity: Design, technology, business, life.* Cambridge, MA: MIT Press.

Schleicher, A. (Ed.). (2011). *Lessons from PISA for the United States: Strong performers and successful reformers in education.* Paris: OECD Publishing. http://dx.doi.org/10.1787/9789264096660-en.

———. (Ed.). (2012). *Preparing teachers and developing school leaders for the 21st century: Lessons from around the world.* Paris: OECD Publishing. http://www.oecd.org/.

Siegel, A., and Etzkorn, I. (2011). *Simple: Conquering the crisis of complexity.* New York: Twelve.

Taylor, F. (1911). *Principles of scientific management.* New York: Harper and Brothers.

Wagner, T., Kegan, R., Lahey, L., Lemons, R. W., Garnier, J., Helsing, D., Rasmussen, H. T., et al. (2006). *Change leadership: A practical guide to transforming our schools.* San Francisco: Jossey-Bass.

Weber, M. (1925). *The theory of social and economic organization* (A. M. Henderson and T. Parsons, Trans.). New York: Free Press.

**3**

# WHAT ARE THE DISPOSITIONS OF CONTEMPORARY EDUCATIONAL LEADERSHIP?

"Intelligent performance is not just an exercise of ability. It is more dispositional in nature in that we must activate abilities and set them in motion. Dispositions concern not only what we can do (our abilities) but what we are actually likely to do." In other words, dispositions must be developed, nurtured, supported and practiced on a regular basis.

—Erskine Dottin, *Dispositions as Habits of Mind* (2010, 12)

**A**s described in the previous two chapters, effective school leadership in the information age requires strong knowledge and understanding of the effects of educational leadership on student learning (see chapter 1), as well as the organizational structure of an agile organization to support school leadership (chapter 2). These two concepts form the foundation of contemporary educational leadership upon which dispositional thinking can be effectively activated. This book proposes five dispositions of leadership needed to ensure that educators and students flourish in the twenty-first century. These five dispositions of leadership are as follows:

1. Thinking and acting interdependently (see chapter 4),
2. Communicating to influence (see chapter 5),
3. Gathering and applying information for change (see chapter 6),
4. Seeking support and feedback for learning (see chapter 7), and
5. Pursuing adaptive competence (see chapter 8).

The following chapters will describe each of these dispositions in depth, providing capabilities for each disposition. First, however, this chapter will explore the meaning and significance of dispositions, how they are acquired, and why they are important. This chapter also describes the importance of dispositions as they pertain to leadership in schools.

## WHAT ARE DISPOSITIONS?

The term *disposition* may be known by many names: inclination, mindset, tendency, propensity, predilection, proneness, habit, characteristic, penchant, capability, aptness, potential, leaning, proclivity, urge, affinity, affection, and so on. They all are aiming in the same direction. Some people say, "She has a sunny disposition." This book refers to *thinking dispositions*— tendencies toward patterns of intellectual behavior.

By definition, a disposition is a habit, a preparation, a state of readiness, or a tendency to act in a specified way. Israeli psychologist Gavriel Salomon (1994) suggests that dispositions do more than describe behavior; they assume a causal function and have an explanatory status. A disposition is a cluster of preferences, attitudes, and intentions, plus a set of capabilities that allow the preferences to become realized in a particular way.

Skillful thinkers, therefore, have both thinking abilities *and* thinking dispositions. The critical thinker who seeks balanced reasons in an argument, for example, should have both the ability and the disposition to do so. Good listeners not only have the skills and abilities to listen well but also are inclined to do so and are alert to situations in which skillful listening presents itself. Ron Ritchhart (2002) defines dispositions as follows:

> Acquired patterns of behavior that are under one's control and will as opposed to being automatically activated. Dispositions are overarching sets of behaviors, not just single specific behaviors. They are dynamic and idiosyncratic in their contextualized deployment rather than prescribed actions to be rigidly carried out. More than desire and will, dispositions must be coupled with the requisite ability. Dispositions motivate, activate, and direct our abilities. (31)

This is interpreted to mean the following:

- *Dispositions are acquired.* People are not necessarily born with them (although the capacity and potential for their acquisition is believed to be innate); rather, they are learned over time. They are repetitive patterns, not single events or skills. They are under an individual's control;

people can consciously, intentionally choose to employ them, rather than them being mindless habits on autopilot.

- *Dispositions are manifested by a complex integration of several skills or behaviors.* Skillful listening, for example, is a complex mix of skills requiring attention to what others are saying, paraphrasing, inquiring, holding our thoughts in abeyance, self-monitoring, taking turns talking, and so forth.
- *There are no recipes, prescribed sequences, or scripts for the actions and behaviors of dispositions.* Rather, they are "maps of the territory" with several pathways leading from where people are to where they hope to be. Furthermore, as individuals become aware that the territory is changing, so too must actions change.
- *Skills, capabilities, and abilities are needed.* Desire and yearning to accomplish some task or master some performance is not enough; individuals must also have the skills, capacities, and abilities to do so.
- *Directing one's abilities implies constant monitoring of actions and comparing them with intentions, values, and desires; that is, "am I behaving consistently, 'walking the talk?'"* Furthermore, what a person is not "up on" they are most likely "down on." Human beings are more likely to act on the beliefs they embrace—they are more likely to be moved to action about passions they hold and more likely to advocate to others what they are skillful at themselves (Costa and Kallick 2008).

## WHY DISPOSITIONS?

Knowledge of methods alone will not suffice; there must be the desire, the will to employ them. This desire is an affair of personal dispositions.

—John Dewey, *How We Think* (1933, 30)

Dispositions not only direct strategic abilities but also help activate relevant content and experiential knowledge by bringing that knowledge to the forefront to better illuminate the situation at hand (Ritchhart 2002). Thinking dispositions develop resourcefulness (capacities) for expanding that knowledge and those skills and capabilities.

Dispositional thinking informs and mediates that knowledge and those skills and capabilities (Feuerstein, Feuerstein, and Falik 2010). Intelligent action in the world is what counts most. Dispositions alert an individual to occasions for the application and the inclination to put skills and knowledge into play. Dispositions become the patterns of a leader's exhibited behavior over time (Davidson 2013).

## DISPOSITIONS FOR EDUCATIONAL LEADERSHIP

Dispositions exhibited by school leaders have a cascading effect throughout the organization. As dispositions are modeled, made explicit, and reflected upon at the administrative level, they are imitated by the teachers who, in turn, model them for their students. Thus, such dispositions as thinking and acting interdependently or communicating to influence soon become norms that are manifested in classrooms and throughout the school organization—they become the way things are done.

The internalization of dispositions is what distinguishes being smart from being wise. Smart people know lots of answers; they may have great stores of knowledge. Wise people possess the disposition and common sense for knowing when and where to use (or not use) that knowledge. Additionally, leaders are alert to a group's performance and advocate for dispositions, capabilities, and practices such as listening with understanding and empathy and collecting data to assist in decision making.

## WHAT ROLES DO DISPOSITIONS SERVE IN LEADERSHIP?

Dispositions increase the likelihood that leaders will respond to problems successfully and become better able to deal with complexities within the organization in the following ways:

- A leader will reframe disappointments as opportunities and look inside the group for internal resources to solve the problem.
- When faced with stubborn problems, a leader will consider various perspectives as part of the problem-solving process.
- A leader will become aware when a plan is not working and, when needed, completely change course during a meeting and invite the group to reset the plan and suggest alternative strategies.
- A leader will work diligently to perfect his or her leadership skills by adapting to and embracing changing demands.
- A leader will regard mission and vision building as collaborative pursuits.

## HOW ARE DISPOSITIONS ACQUIRED?

Human babies learn fast. By the time infants are three months old, their unfinished brains are laced with a trillion connections and these connections triple in a year (Mohan 2013). For example, babies are born with the natural capacity to learn any language. Neuronal connections in their brain are formed through hearing, mimicking, and experimenting with sounds. Through neural pruning, they strengthen their use of the language they hear and give up the sounds and patterns they do not hear.

Likewise, all humans, for example, have a natural capacity for creativity, flexibility, continuous learning, togetherness, wonderment, curiosity, and so forth. The capacities are innate. In their early years, however, if children are criticized for thinking differently, or if their environments are impoverished, such natural capacities may be underdeveloped.

Humans are born with the capacity of curiosity—to question and to explore. Living in a nonresponsive, barren environment and being admonished for asking questions will soon thwart this tendency. On the other hand, when children develop in rich, responsive environments where challenging tasks requiring persistence are given, where children hear complex language, and where children have to solve their own problems, then these capacities are developed more fully and are more likely to continue developing over time.

By interacting with others and with their environment, by observing significant adults who model the dispositions through direct instruction and mediation (Feuerstein, Feuerstein, and Falik 2010), by receiving feedback from others, and by self-observation, these naturally occurring human capacities are expanded and refined over time. Drawing attention to nonexamples, or what dispositions are not, enhances understanding and learning.

## WHY CONSIDER UTILIZING THINKING DISPOSITIONS WITH EDUCATORS?

Education has a weak knowledge base compared to other professions, few required protocols to assist in systematically incorporating best practices, and a reliance on experts dictating to practitioners about best practices (Resnick et al. 2010). This comes as no surprise, since it was asserted in chapter 1 that the relationship between educational leadership and student learning was not researched or well understood until recently.

In addition, as discussed in chapter 2, there has been a historical focus in educational systems on the formal organization that values being rule based and compliant, and does not promote deep thought or problem solving. The historical formal organization has a reliance on veridical decision making based on the identification of the correct responses, with a focus on being independent of the decision maker.

Implementation of new ideas or practices in this environment has had a focus on "what" to implement, with those higher up in the hierarchy telling subordinates what to teach and how to teach. However, implementation and innovation in the information age are not simply technical processes or about having the right idea. They require diagnosing how ideas are formed and how people think, interact, and respond to changes in their learning environment.

The reasons many implementation efforts do not work remain in the realm of *how* to positively influence school culture and in the complex nature of individual and group social interactions. The education profession has far more knowledge about the science of learning than insights into implementing practices informed by the science of learning. Preparing teachers and principals for how to implement requires a change in organizational design, with a focus on thinking, learning, and adaptive competence.

Adaptive competence is the ability to flexibly and creatively apply domain-specific knowledge, utilize metacognitive strategies that were acquired from formal and informal learning situations, and determine how to apply insights in novel or nonroutine settings. Adaptive decision making focuses on how to think about and approach the work and implies less certainty about the ultimate outcome than *what* to do for a planned implementation. Adaptive decision making is actor centered and is guided by an individual's content knowledge, metacognitive capabilities, confidence, emotions, and priorities.

An agile organization, described in chapter 2, distributes leadership throughout a learning community—identified as a network-centric collaborative group—in the form of dispositions of leadership. The five dispositions of leadership noted in figure 3.1 create patterns of thinking, or habits of mind, for use by all members of a learning community.

Activating these dispositions of leadership on a strong foundation of knowledge and understanding of the effect of educational leadership on student learning (see chapter 1), coupled with the support of a redesigned agile organization (see chapter 2), will provide district leaders, principals, and schools with the tools needed to address adaptive challenges in the information age. Adaptive competence and adaptive decision making will

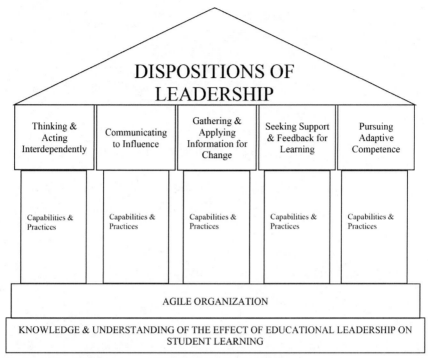

**Figure 3.1.   Dispositions of leadership framework**

be the centerpiece of a network-centric collaborative group for applying current knowledge about teaching and learning, and implementing this knowledge in one's own school culture or novel setting.

A major focus in such a community is developing a learning environment that fosters expert thinking and adaptive competence through the application of dispositions of leadership. Arthur Costa and Bena Kallick (2008) note, "A Habit of Mind is a pattern of intellectual behaviors that leads to productive actions. When we experience dichotomies, are confused by dilemmas, or come face-to-face with uncertainties, and our most effective response requires drawing forth certain patterns of intellectual behavior" (16). In other words, dispositions of leadership are ways of thinking when confronted with complex problems or adaptive challenges.

A term from the maritime community that assists in our understanding the role of applying dispositions of leadership is a peripatetic or "traveling" pivot point that is unique to large ocean-going vessels. A large ship can pivot on any point along the entire length of the ship depending upon wind, vessel speed, tide, current, water displacement, or other forces. The captain's role is to monitor all the forces at play and adapt to the current situation by applying the necessary actions for safely piloting the vessel.

There is not a simple formula for piloting a vessel in the open ocean or leading a school. The unpredictability of ship handling is a helpful analogy for implementing new or innovative ideas in a school system or school that intersects with individual and group social interactions and school culture.

## DISPOSITIONS BUILD THE SCHOOL CULTURE

> Positive dispositions embrace a growth mind set; and schools that support and encourage the use of positive dispositions are more likely to see significant improvement among its teachers and work cultures that support excellence.
>
> —Reuven Feuerstein, Rafael Feuerstein,
> and Louis Falik, *Beyond Smarter* (2010, 14)

Peter Senge and colleagues (2012) suggest that a culture is people thinking together. As individuals share meaning, they negotiate and build a culture. Over time, as leaders employ and display these dispositions, the dispositions begin to pervade the value system, which results in the changing of the norms, practices, and beliefs of the entire organization or group. When leaders model, label, and articulate norms as values and skills, school staff members take collective responsibility for their own and their students' learning. They are no longer "my" students or "your" students; they become "our" students.

By employing the dispositions in the everyday operation of the school, the group mind illuminates issues, solves problems, makes decisions, and accommodates differences. As shared meanings grow, the group builds an atmosphere of trust in human relationships, trust in the processes of interaction, and trust throughout the organization. The common vocabulary, the agreement on the desired attributes of the graduates of the school, the signals in the environment, the rituals and celebration, and the communications and recognitions all facilitate the creation of a shared vision.

## THE FIVE DISPOSITIONS OF LEADERSHIP

The subsequent chapters examine the five dispositions of leadership in a detailed manner with an emphasis on the thinking and the capabilities within each disposition. Robert Kegan and Lisa Lahey (2009) suggest that "when we experience the world as 'too complex' we are not just experiencing the complexity of the world. We are experiencing a mismatch between the world's complexity and our own at this moment. There are only two logical ways to mend this mismatch—reduce the world's complexity or increase our own" (12). Since the world's complexity cannot be reduced, the only viable option is increase one's own.

The five dispositions of leadership act as a schema for developing mental models that assist educators when they encounter the ambiguity of many complex problems. It is helpful to view dispositions in the context of leading schools as "ways of thinking" with capabilities as "ways of being" and practices as "ways of doing." The five dispositions of leadership are thinking and acting interdependently, communicating to influence, gathering and applying information for change, seeking support and feedback for learning, and pursuing adaptive competence. These five aforementioned dispositions were selected because of

- congruence with Kenneth Leithwood and Karen Seashore Louis's (2012) core practices and pathways and Viviane Robinson's (2011) dimensions and capabilities;
- successful implementation by practicing school leaders in high-performing teams and school-based leadership teams;
- suggestions from formative feedback by principals, leadership coaches, and program evaluators; and
- the strategy that a small number of higher-impact dispositions is more likely to be utilized across a school district or school.

The following chapters provide a closer look at each of the five dispositions of leadership, noted in figure 3.1. These dispositions and capabilities provide a structure for congruence between ways of thinking and ways of being. Specific discussion of practices, or ways of doing, are beyond the scope of this book and are described in more detail in a forthcoming book that focuses on practical application of the dispositions of leadership. In addition to the cascading effect noted earlier, leaders who model congruence will establish certainty and predictability for their staffs—two essential components for developing relational trust.

## DISPOSITIONS, CAPABILITIES, AND PRACTICES: WAYS OF THINKING, BEING, DOING

The information age presents leaders with the opportunity to solve complex problems and adaptive challenges that are often unfamiliar and nonroutine. Complex problems and adaptive challenges, by their nature, are not solvable by applying a linear, step-by-step process. These require an approach that equips leaders with the dispositions, capabilities, and practices that interact in an overlapping and interdependent manner, as noted in figure 3.2. We suggest that educational leadership for the information age requires innovative ways of thinking (dispositions), being (capabilities), and doing (practices).

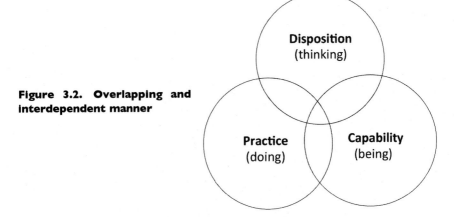

**Figure 3.2. Overlapping and interdependent manner**

Three tendencies in the educational leadership literature influenced the decision to present leadership as the congruence between thinking, being, and doing. The first tendency is to create a list of the practices an effective leader utilizes, with the hope that others might replicate them. It is challenging to replicate leadership practices when the thinking behind how to approach leading is absent.

The second tendency is to discuss the balcony view (see "The Balcony and the Dance Floor" section of this chapter) of leading by identifying desirable leadership attributes such as democratic, authentic, innovative, or transformational. It is difficult to operationalize such broad attributes into realistic capabilities and practices that address a pervasive focus on student learning.

The third tendency is to markedly overemphasize the dance-floor view, or one aspect of leadership, such as the instructional dimension. It can lead to a view of teaching and learning as solely a technical endeavor that can be influenced by simply getting the right curriculum or best practices in place.

The leadership literature reviewed in chapter 1 revealed a need to support school leaders with an approach that incorporates a view from both the balcony and the dance floor. There is also a fluid and interchangeable application in the literature for the terms behaviors, actions, practices, capabilities, responsibilities, and dispositions. The concepts of thinking, being, and doing, linked with corresponding descriptions, resonate with school leaders because they are understandable, practical, and manageable.

## THE BALCONY AND THE DANCE FLOOR

Ron Heifetz (2002) writes of "going to the balcony" to observe with the intention of seeing the broad picture and to carefully diagnose what is needed in the given situation. In contrast, the "dance floor" is working closely, informed by the balcony view, in order to plan, problem solve, and reflect with others. The analogy of the balcony and the dance floor is used here to illustrate the need for moving between assessing a situation and direct involvement in order to influence the work within the school community.

The influential leader will be able to strategically and skillfully move back and forth between the two perspectives in a reciprocal process. The idea of school leaders viewing situations from the balcony and the dance floor begins with diagnosis. What might be needed and how it might be approached is the essence of diagnosing a situation. Diagnosing a situation requires expertise drawn from experience and a skill set for applying useful knowledge learned previously to a new setting.

## SUMMARY

School leaders in the information age are called upon to be adaptively competent—to have the ability to creatively transfer and apply acquired learning in novel or nonroutine settings. Adaptive competence is an ultimate goal of learning for school leaders and a needed alternative to the prescriptive application of others' ideas. The five dispositions of leadership provide a framework for assisting leaders in meeting adaptive challenges within schools, with *pursuing adaptive competence* serving as a keystone disposition.

The dispositions of leadership applied as a framework cannot avert complexities or avoid unpredictable challenges that arise within an educational setting. However, it is possible, by learning new ways of thinking, being, and doing, that a predictable and productive work environment can be created. Colleagues are more likely to follow a leader when a predictable work environment is designed intentionally and there is a perceived congruence between how individuals explain their thinking and how they explain their actions.

In efficacious schools, dispositions, capabilities, and practices are distributed and used by all members within a school community to improve student learning. Robinson (2011) and Leithwood and Seashore Louis (2012) emphasize the importance of distributing leadership, because the expertise needed to influence student learning cannot reside in one person. The heroic leader or a leader-centric model of leadership is no longer sufficient.

Distributing leadership means fostering expertise and capabilities within others. Leadership is minimized when thought of as residing solely within one person designated as the formal leader. Leadership is expanded when thought of as a function and limited when described as a role. Distributing leadership is confused by the many different conceptions of what it means to a school community.

In the introduction, the insights of Wagner and colleagues (2006) identified the challenges of addressing change within the organization and within individuals simultaneously. Many school leaders discover that developing patterns of distributing leadership and simultaneously creating an environment that supports teachers within their school community is an adaptive challenge. Distributing leadership is successful when trust is high and emotions are acknowledged and self-regulated, in order to collaboratively focus on student learning. This delicate and challenging work requires members of a school community to think and act interdependently.

Well-designed structures and routines must be a consideration for many of the capabilities and practices of the five dispositions of leadership to be utilized effectively. For instance, for educators to think and act interdependently, blocks of time must be set aside for discussion or dialogue, and protocols that promote planning, problem solving, and reflecting must be understood and used.

In the following chapters, the dispositions of leadership identified in figure 3.1, will be presented following the pattern of defining the disposition (thinking) and the capabilities (being). Dispositions and capabilities are presented in their entirety. In addition, all the practices are described in detail in the learning guides that accompany training in the five dispositions of leadership.

A vignette based upon more than a decade of work with school leaders was created for each disposition of leadership. The vignettes include one capability and one practice and in most cases discuss structures and routines that are carefully designed for replication by readers. The context of a middle school is used where the principal and school-based leadership team learn together by applying their understanding of dispositions. The nature of the challenges they face grows increasingly complex.

## QUESTIONS TO ENGAGE YOUR THINKING AND DISCUSSION WITH COLLEAGUES

1. If you were to explain a disposition to a colleague, what key ideas might you share?
2. As you confront the ambiguity and complexities of school life as a leader, which of these dispositions might you find useful in your work?

## REFERENCES

Costa, A. L., and Kallick, B. (2008). *Learning and leading with habits of mind: 16 essential characteristics for success*. Alexandria, VA: Association for Supervision and Curriculum Development.

Davidson, C. N. (2013). *Now you see it: How the brain science of attention will transform the way we live, work, and learn*. New York: Viking Press.

Dewey, J. (1933). *How we think*. Boston: Heath.

Dottin, E. (2010). *Dispositions as habits of mind*. Lanham, MD: University Press of America.

Feuerstein, R., Feuerstein, R., and Falik, L. (2010). *Beyond smarter: Mediated learning and the brain's capacity for change*. New York: Teachers College Press.

Heifetz, R. (1994). *Leadership without easy answers*. Cambridge, MA: Belknap Press of Harvard University Press.

Heifetz, R., Linsky, M. (2002). *Leadership on the line: Staying alive through the dangers of leading*. Boston, MA: Harvard Business School Press.

Kegan, R., and Lahey, L. (2009). *Immunity to change: How to overcome it and unlock potential in yourself and your organization*. Boston: Harvard Business Press.

Leithwood, K., and Seashore Louis, K. (2012). *Linking leadership to student learning*. San Francisco: Jossey-Bass.

Mohan, G. (2013, April 21). No kidding: At 5 months babies start to figure it out. *Sacramento Bee*, Health and Science, A9.

Resnick, L. (1999). Making America smarter. *Education Week, Century Series, 18*(40), 38–40.

Resnick, L. B., Spillane, J., Goldman, P., and Rangel, E. (2010). Implementing innovation: From visionary models to everyday practice. In D. Istance, F. Benavides, and H. Dumont (Eds.), *Innovative learning environments*. Paris: Organisation for Economic Co-operation and Development.

Ritchhart, R. (2002). *Intellectual character: What it is, why it matters, and how to get it*. San Francisco: Jossey Bass.

Robinson, V. (2011). *Student-centered leadership*. San Francisco: Jossey-Bass.

Salomon, G. (1994). *Interaction of media, cognition and learning: An exploration of how symbolic forms cultivate mental skills and affect knowledge acquisition*. New York: Routledge.

Senge, P., Cambron-McCabe, N., Lucas, T., Smith, B., Dutton, J., and Kleiner, A. (2012). *Schools that learn (updated and revised): A fifth discipline fieldbook for educators, parents, and everyone who cares about education*. New York: Currency.

Wagner, T., Kegan, R., Lahey, L., Lemons, R. W., Garnier, J., Helsing, D., Rasmussen, H. T., et al. (2006). *Change leadership: A practical guide to transforming our schools*. San Francisco: Jossey-Bass.

# 4

# THINKING AND ACTING
# INTERDEPENDENTLY

Surround yourself with amazingly intelligent men and women. The people I work with not only are smarter than I am, possessing both intellectual and emotional intelligence, but also share my determination to succeed. I will not make an important decision without them.

—George Steinbrenner, former owner of the New York Yankees

In this book, *thinking and acting interdependently* is defined as promoting a positive, collaborative learning culture through distributed leadership. A question in front of educators with this disposition is, what ways of "thinking, being, and doing" would serve schools well as educators work together to create a collaborative environment that is focused on providing a coherent learning experience for students? A collaborative learning culture is defined by the vision, goals, expectations, and norms for adult interactions that support a productive work environment.

Thinking and acting interdependently will be presented as six capabilities in this chapter. They are as follows:

1. establishing and maintaining an environment of trust that includes predictable values and predictable skills;
2. identifying, articulating, and aligning with a shared vision that addresses a pervasive focus on student and adult learning;

3. promoting a group of diverse individuals to access and utilize resources and expertise across a broader community for the benefit of all;
4. setting aside your own preferences;
5. having the capacity to look at things from others' points of view; and
6. anticipating ways to support others in the collaborative process.

All six capabilities noted above are important. However, developing a shared vision is described in more detail than the other five capabilities because of the importance of setting direction for a school district and schools. The idea of developing a community with a shared vision around a limited number of goals that are attainable and realistic is prevalent in the educational leadership literature. Setting direction and influencing others by establishing a pervasive focus on student learning can only be realized in a community that can think and act interdependently.

Many school districts and schools have low levels of commitment and understanding of their shared vision because sequential steps that include goals, action steps, and implications for the learning environment for students and adults are not clear. This chapter outlines the necessary information for developing a shared vision, but not in a prescriptive and rigid manner, so that it can be adapted to numerous school settings. A clear focus leads to understanding expectations and yields higher levels of commitment by principals and teachers.

Effective application of the disposition *thinking and acting interdependently* relies upon many of the topics discussed in "Communicating to Influence" (chapter 5). Successful collaborative cultures are shaped by the established procedures, processes, protocols, and routines that are in place that structure a productive work environment as noted in chapter 5. Readers will realize that the six capabilities noted in this chapter will require the skills of effective communicators, covered in more detail in chapter 5.

## CAPABILITY ONE: ESTABLISHING AND MAINTAINING AN ENVIRONMENT OF TRUST THAT INCLUDES PREDICTABLE VALUES AND PREDICTABLE SKILLS

Trust is an essential component of developing a community. Viviane Robinson (2011) asserts that "in schools with a higher level of trust, teachers experience a stronger sense of professional community and are more willing to innovate and take risks" (34). Leadership hinges upon influence, and the best way to gain influence is for staff members to feel their unique perspectives are understood. Once colleagues feel heard and understood, they are much more likely to follow and to take the leader's direction to heart. When leaders place themselves in their staff members' shoes, it helps the leader make better decisions and earns respect in the long run.

In addition to a stronger sense of professional community, Robinson (2011) also notes, "Students in high-trust schools make more academic and social progress than students in otherwise similar low-trust schools" (34). Earning and maintaining trust in a community is an ongoing day-by-day challenge that Ron Heifetz (1994) contends is a combination of predictable values and predicable skills. Predictable values, such as honesty and integrity, and predictable skills, understood as role competence, need to be present in any community when encouraging individuals to participate.

Similarly, David Rock (2009) suggests that establishing a safe work environment must include certainty and predictability. Communities need trusting relationships when embarking into uncharted territory fraught with complexity that can be both daunting and unnerving. As identified by Kenneth Leithwood and colleagues (2011), addressing the emotions path helps individuals productively respond to their environment. The emotions path is one of the paths that leadership travels within a school community.

As leaders set direction and influence others, careful thought should be given regarding how best to foster trust so that adults in the school can successfully work together while navigating the complex waters of improving student learning. In order to effectively influence the work of individuals or groups, a leader needs a skill set for creating a supportive and productive environment that maintains psychological safety for all participants.

The five dispositions of leadership share practices that overlap. For instance, in building a shared vision, techniques and strategies associated with the disposition *communicating to influence* will be used. Establishing and maintaining an environment requires leaders to model "ways of doing" (practices) that are transparent for adults in the school. A leader establishing a productive work environment will create a sense of psychological safety, encourage balanced participation, and carefully use language by paraphrasing and asking thoughtful questions.

Trust building is a process that takes an enormous investment of time and effort on the part of the leader. There is an investment of time, energy, and skills to establish and maintain trust. Trust is the "glue" that bonds individuals together when deciding on policies and practices that promote the welfare of the students and school improvement strategies. Megan

Tschannen-Moran and Anita Woolfolk Hoy (2001) illuminate such leadership behaviors in creating trust as follows:

- being visible and accessible,
- behaving consistently,
- keeping commitments,
- sharing personal information about out-of-school activities,
- keeping confidences,
- revealing feelings,
- expressing personal interest in other people,
- acting nonjudgmentally,
- listening reflectively,
- admitting mistakes, and
- demonstrating professional knowledge and skills.

Trust grows stronger as long as these behaviors continue, but a relationship can be seriously damaged when someone is discourteous or disrespectful, makes value judgments, overreacts, acts arbitrarily, threatens, or is personally insensitive to others. The most effective strategies for restoring trust include apologizing, asking forgiveness, acknowledging and taking responsibility without making "excuses," and making a commitment to and exploring strategies for preventing the repetition of the behavior in the future. Staff members would rather follow a leader who is always real rather than one who is always right.

Leaders promote personal regard by

- spending time with others and engaging in activities related to out-of-school tasks;
- inquiring about others' personal interests and experiences; and
- practicing such fundamental behaviors as courtesy and respect.

In a busy, task-oriented, sometimes frantic school, these little personal connections are often forgotten or overlooked, resulting in an emotionally barren environment.

## CAPABILITY TWO: IDENTIFYING, ARTICULATING, AND ALIGNING WITH A SHARED VISION THAT ADDRESSES A PERVASIVE FOCUS ON STUDENT AND ADULT LEARNING

Developing a vision, creating goals, and setting direction are important aspects of leading a school district or a school. So much so that developing a shared vision, creating goals, and setting direction are considered a leadership dimension by Robinson (2011) and a core practice by Kenneth Leithwood and Karen Seashore Louis (2012). Leaders within an agile organization recognize that creating a system *focus* is accomplished by developing and communicating district-level goals.

Identifying and articulating a shared vision includes establishing important goals for designing a student-learning environment while creating a sense of urgency for high performance expectations for all students. The term "student-learning environment" is used here to include student achievement as one component because a shared vision should consider all aspects of learning. Student achievement is certainly important to monitor. A student-learning environment is created by integrating the inseparable components of content acquisition, knowledge application, motivation, emotion, and metacognition.

Change also impacts adults significantly in schools. A shared vision wisely recognizes that adult learning needs to be addressed when setting goals. Goal setting often establishes expectations for system outputs, such as student achievement and educator accountability, without the commensurate adjustments to the environment for system inputs, including structures, routines, and learning opportunities. Table 4.1 provides examples of the relationship between establishing system outputs and the system inputs that might be needed.

**Table 4.1.  School system outputs and needed system inputs**

| Setting system outputs established | Setting system inputs needed |
| --- | --- |
| Improved student academic performance | Adjust learning environment to address content knowledge acquisition, as well as application of skills, motivation, emotion, and metacognition. |
| Improved school-level performance | Establish new routines for network-centric collaborative group processes based on relational trust for professional learning opportunities and sharing expertise. |

Thoughtfully constructed group processes are needed in order to develop a shared vision and foster commitment to goals. James Comer and colleagues (1999) noted that collaboration, consensus, and no-fault conversations are essential components of a process for setting goals that are in the best interest of all students. No-fault conversations, the absence of assigning blame, are required if participants are to be encouraged to commit to goals that are set. (For a detailed process for developing a group's shared vision, see chapter 1 in *Schools That Deliver*, by John Edwards and Bill Martin, 2016).

Agreement and consensus, however, are not to be confused with alignment. While a group might make a modest commitment to a vision, the actions and behaviors of each of the members must be in alignment or be congruent with that vision. With alignment, many of the decisions in a school become clear: where and how to expend the limited resources of time, energy, or finances. If the decision is aligned with the shared vision, then it becomes a strong candidate for adoption. If it were not aligned, then it would not be considered, as it would dilute the power of the agreed-upon shared vision.

Such discussion about how decisions, adoptions, or action plans align with the school's vision is healthy. Undermining the shared vision is not healthy (Edwards and Martin 2016). However, it is healthy to explore levels of flexibility and autonomy during the development of school-level goals. There are times that consensus on all goals might not be obtainable, especially when groups are large.

Achieving commitment from all community members is a realistic alternative to obtaining consensus. Patrick Lencioni (2005) asserts that achieving commitment is "about a group of intelligent, driven individuals buying in to a decision precisely when they don't naturally agree. In other words, it's the ability to defy a lack of consensus" (51). Achieving commitment is a helpful notion and is an alternative for groups that are deadlocked and unable to reach consensus.

Developing a shared vision embodies the beliefs and values of a school community. A shared vision is important because it connects people to the work at a meaningful level. A shared vision that addresses our interconnectedness and need for interdependence is more likely to foster acceptance and commitment.

The statements in a shared vision are abstract because they reflect the beliefs and values that focus, connect, and provide purpose for our work. Broad statements in a shared vision need specificity for providing direction and focus for schools. Goal statements provide the specificity for the educators who will do the actual work. Action steps clarify responsibility for implementing goals. Implications for student and adult learning anticipate the needed changes in the learning environment and routines. A shared vision without goals that include action steps can create confusion and result in multiple interpretations for how to move forward.

Figure 4.1 depicts the levels of abstraction for a shared vision based on beliefs and values, associated goals statements, and action steps with the implications for the student and adult learning environment. The pyramid

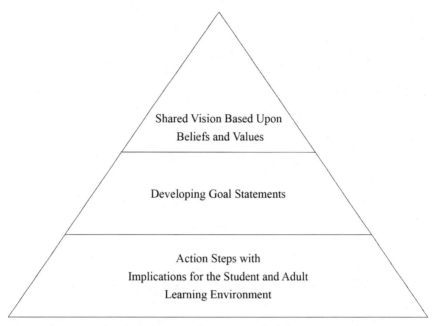

**Figure 4.1.   Levels of abstraction for a shared vision**

intentionally presents the concept of "levels of abstraction." The top section should contain fewer, more abstract statements than the bottom section of the pyramid. If it does not, the result is a shared vision without goals or a focus. The bottom of the pyramid should contain more concrete statements than the top of the pyramid.

The authors have spent decades working in school districts and schools and have facilitated, participated, and witnessed myriad shared-vision and goal-setting processes. It is important in the development of a shared vision that goal statements with action steps that address the learning environment for students and the learning environment and routines for adults are included.

As an example of identifying and articulating a shared vision that addresses a pervasive focus on student and adult learning, textbox 4.1 states the belief that the school system will maintain a pervasive focus on student learning in which all students can learn. A goal that many school districts set that is aligned with this belief is that all primary students should have access to high-quality reading instruction and exit grade 3 reading at grade level. Powerful evidence exists that not reading at level by the end of third grade has dire consequences for a child's educational and social development (Feister 2010).

## Textbox 4.1. Example of a shared vision based on a belief and one goal

**Belief:** Our school system will maintain a pervasive focus on student learning in which all students can learn.
**Goal:** All primary students should have access to high-quality reading instruction and exit grade 3 reading at grade level.

Textboxes 4.2 and 4.3 provide illustrative examples of developing action steps for goal statements, and subsequently identifying and articulating the implications for the student and adult learning environments. Each textbox states a reading action step, notes the implications for the learning environment for students, and notes the learning environment with routines for adults. (*Adults* includes all of the school-based professionals who interact with students.)

Reading action step one (see textbox 4.2) and step two (see textbox 4.3) provide clarity and specifics for the goals of high-quality reading instruction and student performance. Reading step one and reading step two are also placed in a sequence to illustrate the two key ideas. The first idea is to understand the responsibilities of the formal organization and network-centric collaborative groups. The second idea is to identify the implications of technical problems and adaptive challenges.

## Textbox 4.2. Reading action step one with learning environment implications

### Reading Action Step One

Principals ensure that all assessment data are entered accurately into the web portal for student reading program data and the early warning system indicators.

### Learning Environment Implications for Student Learning

Meaningful reading data are collected for all students. Data are collected in a manner that is least impactful on student learning time. Students are aware of data collected and have an understanding of how they can improve their performance.

### Learning Environment Implications for Adult Learning and Routines

#### Adult Learning

Teachers have knowledge of what reading data are collected and understand how to interpret the results. Teachers have been trained in the data web portal system and how to use it effectively. Data are used as a tool for making program and instructional adjustments.

#### Routines

The data web portal system is easy to access, and computers are readily available for data entry.

Earlier in the book, the assertion was made that leaders in an agile organization clearly identify the responsibilities of the formal organization and those of network-centric collaborative groups. The responsibilities for leaders of the formal organization, or school district, are system-centric and must be in place for work to be accomplished at the school level.

Reading action step one in textbox 4.2 suggests that the principal ensures all assessment data is entered into the web portal. The district leadership is responsible for a functional and useable web-based data system, computers for data entry, and training for principals and teachers for entering data and interpreting results in reading action step one. Reading action step one presents mostly technical problems, as opposed to adaptive challenges, with the formal organization assuming much of the responsibility for implementation.

Reading action step two in textbox 4.3 states that principals and teachers use assessment data for reading placement and decisions to make adjustments to program and instruction. Reading action step two presents both technical problems and adaptive challenges. The formal organization, or district leadership, is responsible for the technical aspects of reading action step one by providing research-based reading materials and time in elementary schools for a ninety-minute reading block. The ongoing professional learning for high-quality reading instruction and training are also district or formal organization responsibilities.

## Textbox 4.3. Reading action step two with learning environment implications

**Reading Action Step Two**

Principals and teachers systematically and routinely use assessment data by establishing specific times and dates to review the decisions about student placement and adjustments to student program needs in reading.

**Learning Environment Implications for Student Learning**

Students are placed accurately in setting using research-based reading materials. A ninety-minute reading block is a routine part of a reading system. The five essential elements of reading are utilized during the reading block. Reading interventions are designed and used to assist students with specific reading support. Additional reading support personnel assist students based on reading assessment data. Summer reading programs are available to address summer learning loss.

**Adult Learning**

Teachers have been trained in the district's research-based program materials and have expertise in utilizing the five essential components of reading. Teachers and the principal have been trained in group processes and protocols to have student data meetings that are efficient, effective, and focused on students. Teachers have been trained to understand the level of flexibility, collaboration, and interdependence needed to make program and instructional adjustments to meet the needs of all students in reading.

**Routines**

Teachers and the principal meet regularly and systematically in grade-level data meetings to assess student progress. Grade-level data meetings are established to carefully monitor student reading progress and adjustments are made based upon reading assessments. Flexible instructional groups for core reading and interventions are created by the teachers and adjustments made on student progress.

The learning environment implications for adult learning and routines noted in textbox 4.3 present adaptive challenges as opposed to technical problems for many teachers. A student-focused data team is an example of a network-centric collaborative group in action and assumes much of the responsibility for the implementation of reading action step two.

The team will need to use data to make adjustments to reading program placement, flexible student grouping, and instructional strategies for specific groups of students. The student-focused data team needs to function as a network-centric collaborative group that is trust based, information enabled, and collaborative. This collaborative team effort will require effective group process skills, high levels of cooperation, and thinking interdependently.

In providing technical assistance for state departments of education and numerous school districts, the authors have concluded that failure to attain goals at the school level can often be linked to a failure to understand or address changes needed in the student and adult learning environments. The authors' technical assistance work has been in the field with practitioners in struggling schools with poor student performance. The support of practitioners is rhetorical and symbolic and leads to lack of commitment when a shared vision is developed without addressing responsibility for implementation and needed resources.

An understanding of the responsibilities for implementation of the goals and actions steps by the district-level and school-level leadership provides clarity and organizational focus. However, it enhances commitment and interdependent thinking when a shared vision, goal statements, and action steps are developed collaboratively while noting needed adjustments to the learning environment for student and adults.

## CAPABILITY THREE: PROMOTING A GROUP OF DIVERSE INDIVIDUALS TO ACCESS AND UTILIZE RESOURCES AND EXPERTISE ACROSS A BROADER COMMUNITY

School-district-designed high-performing teams of principals and school-based leadership teams are two examples of network-centric collaborative groups that utilize resources and expertise across a broader community. Strategically using resources is often described in terms of carefully utilizing financial assets and personnel. Resources include the educator expertise, routines, processes, and structures that can be networked across a system to promote improved student learning.

High-performing principal teams and school-based leadership teams are created as district-level practices that address the need for collaborating on common work and developing the capacities to advance a student-learning agenda. Textbox 4.4 identifies relevant recommendations suggested by Kyla Wahlstrom and colleagues (2010, 216) for district practices that support the rationale for creating high-performing teams and school-based leadership teams to focus on student learning.

## Textbox 4.4. Implications for district practice

Be crystal clear and repetitive when communicating the district's agenda for student learning.

Provide increased opportunities for administrators to collaborate on common work.

Provide a wide range of intensive opportunities for teachers and school-level leaders to develop the capacities they need to accomplish the district's student-learning agenda.

Support principals, particularly those new to the district or school, in providing aligned forms of leadership distribution that build on existing strengths.

Provide assistance for teachers and school-level leaders in accessing, interpreting, and making use of evidence for their decisions about teaching and learning.

Network-centric collaborative groups are designed to engage adults in meaningful and demanding work. Anthony Bryk (2015) suggests that networks focused on improving teaching and sharing expertise are needed and not limited to one's brick-and-mortar location: "If educators joined together in structured improvement networks, our field would have extraordinary capacities to innovate, test, and rapidly spread effective practices. . . . Working together and learning together will make it possible to accomplish much more for many more than ever before" (475).

Network-centric collaborative groups that seek to improve teaching will need to be trust-based, flexible, information-enabled, and bound by collaborative norms of behavior. The desire to improve student learning—a professional obligation of all educators—resonates with members of network-centric collaborative groups committed to one another. The creation of high-performing principal teams and school-based leadership teams will not succeed in a formal organization that is focused only on system-centric attributes such as being rule-based and hierarchical, with information controlled tightly.

## CAPABILITY FOUR: SETTING ASIDE YOUR OWN PREFERENCES FOR THE BENEFIT OF ALL

Conceptually, thinking and acting interdependently seems reasonable. Practically, group cohesion can be challenging when each individual must assess what to give up for the benefit of a coherent system for students. Altruism is the human capacity to give up personal goals and instead to work toward the beneficial goals of the group, that is, being willing to sacrifice for the group's benefit. Leaders build trust by publicly expressing feelings and demonstrating behaviors that show a desire to help other people and a lack of their own selfishness. Suspending ego preferences is difficult and is at the core of addressing adaptive challenges.

Heifetz (1994) provides the insight that it is often a temporary sense of loss of identity, competence, or confidence that influences how individuals respond to change. The process of suspending preferences must include a clear understanding of the alternatives to what is in place currently. Leading this process requires a working environment that is supportive, positive, and focused on fostering new learning as well as new patterns of behavior.

## CAPABILITY FIVE: HAVING THE CAPACITY TO LOOK AT THINGS FROM OTHERS' POINTS OF VIEW

The capacity to see things from another person's point of view requires cognitive flexibility. It takes the deliberate, conscious decision to enter another's life and attempt to view a situation or problem from their perspective. It means "walking in their shoes"—entering their emotions and their mind to perceive as they might. It requires the skills of listening with understanding and empathy and the practical skills of paraphrasing and posing questions.

As part of this process, it is essential to build positive relations with others. Stephen Covey (1989) popularized the idea that a habit that should be internalized is seeking to understand others before seeking to be understood. Individuals in a collaborative learning culture make the group decision to seek to understand each other and internalize the behavioral pattern, responding and posing thought-provoking questions in their daily interactions (Costa and Garmston 2015; Garmston and Wellman 2016).

Empathy is the ability to identify and understand another's situation, feelings, concerns, and motives. It means seeing through someone else's eyes. In the demanding, complex, tiring, often-frustrating life of schools, empathy shown by leaders is particularly critical. This doesn't mean that a leader always agrees with others' points of view, nor should leaders try to please everybody. Rather, they take into account staff members' feelings, along with other factors, in the process of making thoughtful decisions.

## CAPABILITY SIX: ANTICIPATING WAYS TO SUPPORT OTHERS IN THE COLLABORATIVE PROCESS

The capability of anticipating ways to support others in the collaborative process includes the reality of how a workday is structured. Leaders within an agile organization understand that collaboration combines a clear student-learning agenda, time reserved for meeting as groups, and individuals trained in skillful ways to interact. Anticipating ways to support others in the collaborative process is essential to effective school leadership.

Historically, in the United States, the education system has been structurally aligned to promote independence within classrooms and schools. School-level autonomy for principals and classroom-level autonomy for teachers has been a well-established cultural value in the United States. Dan Lortie (2002) made two important observations during his research in the 1970s. First, "schools were organized around teacher separation rather than teacher interdependence" (14). Second, "the workplace of the teacher—the school—is not organized to promote inquiry or build the intellectual capital of the occupation" (56).

Mona Mourshed, Chinezi Chijioke, and Michael Barber (2007) note that teachers in most schools in the United States work alone without the benefit of planning or feedback from colleagues. They suggest that the highest-performing school systems in the world "create a culture in their schools in which collaborative planning, reflection on instruction, and peer coaching are the norm and constant features of school life. This enables teachers to develop continuously" (28).

Solving educational problems has become so complex that we need access to all the diverse points of view that we can collect in order to make critical decisions. Practicing ways to think interdependently—to join others in the consideration of important ideas—is one of the most important dispositions of leaders. Global interdependence is made possible through key players who are able to use their social brains to protect and foster the survival needs we now face. Leaders know that while it is important to know how to work effectively when alone, working in groups is more than cooperation.

Thinking interdependently requires leaders to justify ideas and allows them to be open to the ideas of others. Leaders need to test the feasibility of solutions they pose by hearing what others think. They need to be willing and open to feedback from their trusted staff. Through this interaction, the group and the individuals continue to grow. Listening, consensus seeking, giving up an idea to work with someone else's, empathy, compassion, group leadership, knowing how to support group efforts, and altruism—all are behaviors indicative of those who profit from thinking interdependently.

## SUMMARY

A school community that values thinking and acting interdependently fosters "we-ness" as much as "me-ness." Everyone benefits from participating in and contributing to ideas, innovations, and problem solving. Learning unfolds within social contexts, hence interdependence increases collective intelligence. Interdependent people envision the expanding capacities of the group and its members, and they draw on the resources of others to enhance personal competencies. As Margaret Mead is quoted as saying, "Never doubt that a small group of thoughtful, committed citizens can change the world; indeed, it's the only thing that ever has."

Thinking and acting independently should be focused on a student-learning agenda, as well as on a positive collaborative learning culture that enables all educators to develop continuously. In their district-level leadership research, Timothy Waters and Robert Marzano (2006) identified that "defined autonomy" positively influences student learning when principals are expected to *"lead within the boundaries defined by district goals"* (13).

Thinking and acting interdependently is not a call to eliminate independence, defined as the flexibility needed for innovation, or to limit creative thinking to solve complex problems. The collaborative learning culture should focus on the capabilities and practices that support leadership in school systems and schools (Costa and O'Leary 2013). The six capabilities and practices of thinking and acting interdependently should be balanced with recognition of individuality and a process that articulates "defined autonomy."

## MIDDLE SCHOOL VIGNETTE

Sunnydale Middle School is located outside of Chicago and serves a population of students from diverse linguistic and cultural backgrounds. JoAnna became the school principal three years ago. She taught in the district for eleven years before becoming the principal at Sunnydale. JoAnna soon realized that the job of a principal was at times both challenging and rewarding.

JoAnna is impressed with the academic results that the school had produced before she arrived. However, the school superintendent, influenced by expectations of greater accountability, desires increased levels of achievement for all students. The certified staff of forty-one seems to have strong professional relationships and work together in the best interest of their students.

Through analyzing student performance data, the staff noticed that 40 percent of the sixth-grade class was receiving Ds or Fs. When considering what might be causing some students difficulty, the staff noticed that each classroom used a different system for organizing assignments and handling late work. Teachers functioned independently when designing their organizational system. As a result, the staff decided to explore possibilities of designing a consistent system for students.

The school principal recognized the need to support teachers in developing a better process across all classrooms. In order to foster collective problem solving, the principal anticipated ways to support the staff during the collaborative process. For example, during the sixth-grade team meeting, JoAnna spoke to the idea of thinking and acting interdependently in order to accomplish the development of a seamless system for students.

She began by discussing the idea of equal status, effective ways of interacting, and maintaining an environment of trust. She also articulated the shared goal of improved student performance and the commitment to working collaboratively to find solutions to complex problems. Finally, JoAnna emphasized that the goal of the work would be to share knowledge, expertise, and wisdom, and to engage in complex problem solving related to student learning.

During collaboration, teachers identified the following potential causes for the high percentage of sixth-grade students with Ds and Fs:

- Every teacher used a different organizational system for turning in homework, turning in late work, tracking assignments, taking notes, and so forth.
- A five-period day requires students to rapidly adjust to each teacher's requirement for organizing student work and so forth.
- Struggling students are faced with the task of learning academic content as well as learning what each teacher expects in terms of the system for organizing work.

Realizing that the current system did not create coherence for students, teachers suspended preferences for their personal systems, while working collaboratively to develop one approach that would be used by all teachers. Most teachers had to abandon their current approach in order for the new process to be put in place. Personal preferences were set aside, and a diverse set of individuals constructed a school-wide process that benefitted students. This type of collaboration required thinking and acting interdependently in order to accomplish the development of a seamless student feedback system.

## QUESTIONS TO ENGAGE YOUR THINKING AND DISCUSSION WITH COLLEAGUES

1. As you reflect on the ideas of thinking and acting interdependently, what are some issues where there is a need to set aside professional preferences in order to create a more coherent learning system for students?
2. What specific strategies or practices from the disposition of thinking and acting interdependently might you use to encourage a group to reach commitment about an issue in your school?

## REFERENCES

Bryk, A. (2015). 2014 AERA distinguished lecture: Accelerating how we learn to improve. *Educational Researcher, 44*(9), 467–477.

Comer, J. P., Ben-Avie, M., Haynes, N. M., and Joyner, E. T. (1999). *Child by child: The Comer process for change in education.* New York: Teachers College Press.

Costa, A., and Garmston, R. (2015). *Cognitive coaching: Developing self-directed leaders and learners* (3rd Ed.). Lanham, MD: Rowman & Littlefield.

Costa, A., and O'Leary, P. W. (2013). *The power of the social brain.* New York: Teacher College Press.

Covey, S. (1989). *Principle-centered leadership.* New York: Simon and Schuster.

Edwards, J., and Martin, W. (2016). *Schools that deliver.* San Francisco: Corwin.

Feister, L. (2010). *Early warning! Why reading by the end of third grade matters.* Baltimore: Annie E. Casey Foundation.

Garmston, R., and Wellman, B. (2016). *Adaptive schools: A sourcebook for developing collaborative groups.* (3rd Ed.). Lanham, MD: Rowman & Littlefield.

Heifetz, R. (1994). *Leadership without easy answers.* Cambridge, MA: Belknap Press of Harvard University Press.

Leithwood, K., Anderson, S., Blair, M., and Strauss, T. (2011). School leaders' influence on student learning: The four paths. In T. Bush, L. Bell, and D. Middlewood (Eds.), *The principles of educational leadership and management* (pp. 13–30). Thousand Oaks, CA: Sage.

Leithwood, K., and Seashore Louis, K. (2012). *Linking leadership to student learning*. San Francisco: Jossey-Bass.

Lencioni, P. (2005). *Overcoming the five dysfunctions of a team: A field guide*. San Francisco: Jossey-Bass.

Lortie, D. C. (2002). *Schoolteacher: A sociological study*. Chicago: University of Chicago Press.

Mourshed, M., Chijioke, C., and Barber, M. (2007). *How the world's best-performing school systems come out on top*. Chicago: McKinsey.

Robinson, V. (2011). *Student-centered leadership*. San Francisco: Jossey-Bass.

Rock, D. (2009). *Your brain at work: Strategies for overcoming distraction, regaining focus, and working smarter all day long*. New York. HarperCollins.

Tschannen-Moran, M., and Hoy, A. W. (2001). Teacher efficacy: Capturing an elusive construct. *Teaching and Teacher Education, 17*, 783–805.

Wahlstrom, K., Seashore Louis, K., Leithwood, K., and Anderson, S. (2010). *Investigating the links to improved student achievement: Final report of research findings*. Minneapolis: University of Minnesota.

Waters, T. J., and Marzano, R. J. (2006). *School district leadership that works: The effect of superintendent leadership on student achievement*. Denver: McREL.

# 5

# COMMUNICATING TO INFLUENCE

Watch your thoughts, they become words.
Watch your words; they become actions.
Watch your actions; they become habits.
Watch your habits; they become character.
Watch your character; it becomes your destiny.

—Frank Outlaw

**K**enneth Leithwood and Karen Seashore Louis (2012) found that the influence of leadership on student learning is *mostly indirect*. However, the influence of leadership on adult learning should be *mostly direct*. This influence on adults occurs through the medium of effective communication. Leaders who skillfully teach and model effective interpersonal communication and organize network-centric collaborative groups will intentionally and directly influence adult learning. The work of improving student learning, a major responsibility of network-centric collaborative groups, is enhanced when group members use effective communication skills and strategies.

The disposition of *communicating to influence* is defined as developing the interpersonal skills to motivate and mobilize both individuals and groups. This chapter will explore the capabilities of communicating to influence, capabilities designed for use by school leaders and network-centric collaborative groups. Communicating to influence will be presented as four capabilities in this chapter. They are as follows:

1. developing the capabilities within others to interact successfully;
2. developing personal presence;
3. knowing when and why to integrate and knowing when to insert oneself; and
4. using interpersonal skills to cultivate working relationships and to motivate and mobilize others (individuals and groups).

## CAPABILITY ONE: DEVELOPING THE CAPABILITIES WITHIN OTHERS TO INTERACT SUCCESSFULLY

The information age presents the need for designing work environments that support addressing adaptive challenges, solving complex problems, and fostering continuous learning for adults. This is major departure from the industrial age, when a manager might have learned skills to communicate in order to *direct others*. School leaders often find they are unprepared for and overwhelmed by the challenges of organizing and working with groups.

Human emotion, often ignored or separated from cognition, is now at the forefront for leaders to acknowledge and understand. Leithwood (2011) indicates that the rational and emotional dimensions are far more connected than many leaders realize. Leaders willing to create network-centric collaborative groups capable of being member directed need a contemporary understanding of the neuroscience and research that supports designing productive work environments.

A productive and positive work setting has elements of a holding environment, the practices informed by the neuroscience of human social behavior. Donald Winnicott (1960) suggested that holding creates a safe and predictable environment for an infant. A holding environment is constructed so group members feel emotionally safe and capable of engaging in work that might lead to discomfort. A holding environment for adults focuses on the properties that assist individuals and groups in engaging productively while doing challenging work (Heifetz 1994).

Placing emotion in a positive context allows individuals and groups to engage in complex cognitive work. Emotion plays an important role when learning new cognitive information necessitates changes in beliefs and behaviors. Leaders seeking to design a work environment that is intentional about the role of emotion and cognition are well served by understanding the motivation that drives most social interactions.

Evian Gordon (2000) identified that the desire of humans to minimize threat and maximize reward are powerful human motivators. David Rock (2009), informed by the work of Gordon, developed a framework grounded in neuroscience that leaders should utilize when designing processes that involve social interaction. Table 5.1 depicts Rock's SCARF model, comprised of the five domains of status, certainty, autonomy, relatedness, and fairness that influence social interactions. Individuals make frequent assessments about whether to be engaged or disengaged in activities or processes based upon their perception of the domains of SCARF.

**Table 5.1.  The domains of SCARF**

| Domain | Summary |
| --- | --- |
| Status | Our perceived importance to other people and where we rank |
| Certainty | Our ability to predict the future and know what is coming up |
| Autonomy | Our sense of control over situations or events and if we have choice |
| Relatedness | Our feelings of safety with others and whether someone is friend or foe |
| Fairness | Our perception about exchanges between people being fair and equitable |

Source: D. Rock (2009), *Your brain at work: Strategies for overcoming distraction, regaining focus, and working smarter all day long* (New York. HarperCollins).

The domains of SCARF activate either primary reward or primary threat circuitries of the brain. For example, a grade-level or department work group in a school that encourages contributions by early career and veteran teachers alike acknowledges that the status of all participants is equal and important. David Rock and Christine Cox (2012) suggest, "The SCARF model improves people's capacity to understand and ultimately modify their own and other people's behavior in social situations, to thus be more adaptive" (1).

Leaders hoping to design effective work groups might consider the collective IQ insights of Anita Woolley and colleagues (2010). Collective intelligence exists for groups of people and, interestingly, does not strongly correlate with the individual intelligence of group members. Group satisfaction, group cohesion, and group motivation are not correlated with the collective intelligence of a group (688). Woolley and colleagues indicate the three areas that do correlate highly with collective IQ are the average social sensitivity of group members, the equality in distribution of conversational turn taking, and the proportion of females in the group.

Anita Woolley and Thomas Malone (2011) suggest that it is important to have men and women who are high in social sensitivity for groups to enhance decision making and solve complex problems. Attributes of socially sensitive people are the ability to understand and empathize with the thoughts and feelings of others, good listening skills, and openness to the ideas of others. Groups increase the odds of addressing adaptive challenges and solving complex problems when they promote positive social interaction, minimize threat, maximize reward, and apply the techniques and strategies that increase their collective IQ.

Discussion and dialogue are two forms of conversation that groups can select depending on the desired outcome for a meeting. Many groups are not skilled at conversation and often drift between forms of discussion and dialogue only to confuse and frustrate participants. It is helpful for a work group to be aware, understand, and utilize the practices for engaging in dialogue or discussion. Effective work groups learn to be intentional and select the form of conversation that will assist in achieving successful interactions and accomplishing the goals they set.

## Discussion

Discussion is the most common form of group conversation. Discussion is used to propose solutions, make decisions, and select actions. Discussion, by nature, is a convergent process that eliminates choices in order to move forward with a focus. The elements of effective meetings are introduced intentionally within discussion because most meetings that are held in schools are discussions.

Work groups seeking to be efficient and effective create working agreements, use meeting standards, utilize facilitation skills, routinely use a planning template (table 5.2), and identify decision-making authority. Effective work groups design working agreements or expectations that are agreed upon to help the group achieve its purposes. A working agreement is informal and establishes guidelines for how a group wants to work together. A working agreement is developed by the group, is simple and direct, and has a limited number of guidelines.

For example, a grade-level team might need guidelines in their working agreement about starting on time, ending on time, and being on task to enhance team performance. All group members should have a copy and the agreement should be reviewed periodically, or when group membership changes.

Effective groups also use a format for planning a meeting, with the first step of identifying clearly the task or outcome that is desired. A second step is identifying the configuration that will arrange participants into a format that is consistent with the task. The third step is selecting protocols and processes that will lead to accomplishing the outcome or task. Effective groups develop a "bank" of protocols and processes that support a working agreement, such as turn-taking procedures and managing time to encourage balanced participation for making decisions.

Many successful groups utilize protocols and processes so interactions between members purposefully incorporate the domains of SCARF. Successful meetings involve reaching an understanding about accomplishments, assuming responsibility for the next steps that are needed, and reflecting on the interactions and meeting outcomes. Groups need to reflect about the processes used and products produced in order to learn and improve.

**Table 5.2.  Meeting planning format**

| 1. Task or desired outcome | 2. Group configuration options | 3. Process/protocol options |
|---|---|---|
| Briefly describe what it is you hope to accomplish with the meeting. | • Learning pairs<br>• Triads, trios<br>• Learning team: 4 to 6 members<br>• Grade level<br>• Subject area<br>• Cross team (grade or subject)<br>• Cross team with specialists<br>• Self-selected | • Structured dialogue<br>• Chalk talk<br>• Points of most significance<br>• Round robin (one minute)<br>• Round robin (only speak once)<br>• First turn/last turn<br>• Inside/outside circle<br>• Concept attainment<br>• 2 to 4 to 8<br>• Carousel<br>• Whip around |

## Dialogue

Dialogue is used to explore thinking, inquire into the beliefs and values that motivate the work of group members, and assist in understanding one another. Dialogue, by nature, is a divergent process that explores choices and options, and is not bound by making a decision. Dialogue is a conversation type that is underutilized and poorly implemented in many school settings.

Groups that encounter adaptive challenges and complex problems need to view dialogue as an essential process that helps them explore ideas, options, and potential solutions. The manner in which members learn to explore thinking through dialogue is an indication that a group is prepared for addressing the work-related challenges of the information age.

Nancy Dixon (1998) observes that dialogue is a specific form of talk and can be accomplished through three different areas: the skillfulness of participants, the skillful design for encouraging desired interactions, and the way in which participants relate to one another. How conversations are structured, verbal skillfulness, and the manner in which participants regard one another will influence whether a group can explore how to solve complex problems and address adaptive challenges.

Work groups will be needed to select an approach to dialogue by relying on communication skills, a skillful design, relationships of the participants, or elements from all three areas. For most work groups, it is unrealistic to have all members trained initially in skillful verbal techniques that support dialogue.

Dialogue is a type of conversation or talk in which the purpose is for participants to examine assumptions and construct new meaning. Learning new communication skills is important and can enhance the quality of dialogue. However, the nature of the relationship among participants might be the most important factor.

Dixon (1998) suggests that dialogue is "not a difference in technique but a difference in relationship" (61). Therefore, successful dialogue is nonjudgmental, nonevaluative, and nonhierarchical. Dialogue is a foundational process, and when it leads to mutual understanding, especially if student learning is the centerpiece, students served will benefit.

There are two specific actions that a work group can take to establish dialogue as a form of talk. First, utilize norms of interaction that both encourage the use of verbal skillfulness and promote positive relationships. Second, select and begin to build a repertoire of protocols and processes that provide structure and support for the group.

One important feature of dialogue is the intention of *not* making a decision, yet it is having a destination: sensemaking. Karl Weick (1995) suggests that sensemaking is placing items or experiences into a framework by constructing meaning for creating a mutual understanding. Many school districts and schools swim in a sea of initiatives, policies, and programs that few in the organization can fully comprehend due to lack of time or meaningful processes to make sense of it all.

Sensemaking has two important components. First, it is a process for participants to describe clearly and understand the elements of a complex challenge. Participants engaged in sensemaking must avoid offering interpretations of experiences or information. Second, it serves as a catalyst for moving forward. Karl Weick, Kathleen Sutcliffe, and David Obstfeld (2005) note that sensemaking "involves turning circumstances into a situation that is comprehended explicitly in words and that serves as a springboard into action" (409).

The authors have observed two common pitfalls that suggest groups need both steps in the sensemaking process. One pitfall is failure by individuals and the group to describe and understand clearly the complex problem before taking action. A second pitfall is to explore a complex problem without resolution to either forgo a decision or take action as a group. Disillusionment can happen if a group crafts an inadequate solution for a poorly understood challenge or lacks resolution by ongoing dialogue without eventually describing a path forward.

The industrial age notion that new information is interchangeable and can replace old information, without a sensemaking process, by simply inserting it in the organization is still omnipresent in school systems. An entry point for utilizing sensemaking in a school is initiating a dialogue process among the staff that begins first with making sense of the existing web of all programs, resources, and initiatives.

Robert Garmston and Bruce Wellman (2013) have written extensively about the skills and techniques that groups need for successful interpersonal interactions. Their seven norms of collaboration, noted in table 5.3, were developed so groups might be equipped to engage in both dialogue and discussion. Interestingly, the norms of collaborations are consistent with the domains of SCARF, strategies that enhance collective IQ and con-

**Table 5.3. The seven norms of collaboration**

| Norm | Summary |
| --- | --- |
| Pausing | before responding or asking a question allows time for thinking. |
| Paraphrasing | assists members of the group in hearing and understanding one another. |
| Posing questions | to explore and to specify thinking. |
| Putting ideas on the table | is at the heart of meaningful dialogue and discussion. |
| Providing data | supports group members in constructing shared understanding. |
| Pay attention to self and others | to know what is being said, how it is said, and how others are responding. |
| Presuming positive intentions | encourages meaningful dialogue and discussion. |

*Source:* R. Garmston and B. Wellman (2016), *The adaptive school: A sourcebook for developing collaborative groups* (Lanham, MD: Rowman & Littlefield).

tain elements for designing dialogue as noted by Dixon (1998). The norms of collaboration are also useful for discussions.

The responsibility of teaching and modeling communication techniques so adults develop the capabilities and practices to interact successfully is challenging because of the extensive repertoire needed by all the school staff. A school leader must be willing to have effective communication practices taught as well as modeled while interacting one-on-one and in public. Leaders often fall short in the eyes of colleagues because of a lack of congruence between the espoused goal of utilizing effective communication and actual practices.

Interestingly, distributing leadership capabilities and practices frequently begins with a willingness to accept that other colleagues possess talents that a leader may not have. Rather than view this from a personal deficient perspective, it is actually an opportunity to view staff interactions from the balcony while colleagues lead or demonstrate effective communication practices. Who demonstrates effective communication is less important than having the desired practices widespread and modeled consistently. This requires disciplining oneself to manage the impulsivity of wanting to be in charge and control meetings.

Developing the capabilities within others to interact successfully means a shift in role for school leaders. The shift is away from being the band director and toward a music composer creating a score where all instruments are integrated into the music. School leaders assist groups by providing resources, in the form of models, practices, routines, and structures for successful group interactions.

Attempting to control all meetings, or working on the dance floor constantly, denies work groups the opportunity to practice specific techniques and develop a process for feedback from participating members. It is challenging, and for most leaders nearly impossible, to "run" a meeting and assess the resources a work group needs simultaneously.

The choice between the view from the balcony and action on the dance floor is never a simple decision. However, a leader must decide the best course of action that will influence an entire school or a work group in the long term. Work groups will get off task, not follow the norms of collaboration, and ignore their working agreements. The view from the balcony allows a school leader, or a work group leader, to assess group interactions and, if necessary, intervene in the form of reframing interactions.

## CAPABILITY TWO: DEVELOPING PERSONAL PRESENCE

Personal presence involves having heightened levels of self-awareness and social awareness because human interactions are dynamic and situational. Educators must learn to prioritize and identify the communication that is most important and select the time and place for best delivery. An initial step as an effective communicator is to develop personal presence by creating routines and conditions for being calm and focused in social settings.

Effective communicators strive to be calm in preparation for an upcoming interaction or when transitioning from an emotionally taxing situation. An attribute of effective communicators is they "read" situations, make necessary adjustments in the moment, and select from an extensive repertoire of interpersonal skills and strategies.

Two important factors that influence our ability to communicate are informed by neuroscience. First, we really cannot multitask. John Medina (2008) observes that multitasking is possible only with very simple tasks and humans are not capable of attending to two difficult tasks simultaneously. Therefore, effective communicators attend intently to the speaker, listen to understand, and are capable of paraphrasing their thoughts.

Second, Daniel Levitin (2014) observes that the decision-making network of our brain cannot prioritize, has attentional restrictions, and fatigues easily, impacting the quality of our communication. We simply need to recognize that being selective and prioritizing our interactions is necessary because we have neural limitations. Challenging work environments present interpersonal demands that often exceed our ability to communicate effectively.

Maintaining a personal presence in social settings can be inhibited by becoming defensive or taking criticism too personally. It is difficult, especially for inexperienced leaders, to develop strategies for letting go of comments made by others that are not useful in the moment.

There are two helpful approaches that avoid the common interpersonal pitfall of conversations devolving into unproductive, negative, or heated exchanges. First, focus initially on creating an understanding rather than striving to justify, persuade, convince, or convert others to adopt one's point of view. Creating an understanding is about listening to others' thoughts and inquiring to discern what might be the beliefs or values that inform their point of view.

The interpersonal communication skills of pausing, paraphrasing, and inquiring into the thinking of others are tools for maintaining positive and open communication. Fortunately, there is almost always time to craft a thoughtful response, and reminding oneself of this simple fact might inhibit an impulsive and regrettable comment.

Second, in public life we need to recognize that being liked by everyone is unrealistic and a bar set too high. Learning to live with the knowledge that some people will not like us, or might even attempt to undermine our efforts simply because we are in a role of authority, is difficult. The disposition of communicating to influence compels us to take the high road and focus on what will positively influence others.

Decades of experience teaching and supervising school leaders suggests performance as a leader is often judged by how well one maintains a positive personal presence with individuals and groups. Personal presence is maintaining poise and calm while managing our emotions and impulses to react or respond.

## CAPABILITY THREE: KNOWING WHEN AND WHY TO INTEGRATE AND KNOWING WHEN TO INSERT ONESELF

The essence of seeking either the balcony view or the dance-floor view is knowing when and why to integrate into a group and knowing when to insert oneself into a situation. A first step is diagnosing what might be best to help an individual or a group. This prevents the urge to react in the moment and focuses on long-term development through building resourcefulness.

It is a natural inclination, particularly for educators drawn to a helping profession, to want to assist or fix a situation for an individual or a group. Certainly, there are times immediate intervention is warranted when interactions might damage relationships. Whether to integrate by observing and assuming the role of a participant or by intervening begins with a framework for thinking and guiding the decision.

Table 5.4 establishes a framework for guiding a decision to integrate into the group or intervene. This framework will be used to explore interactions with groups. (The table can also be used to explore interactions with individuals.) Effective teachers frequently use criteria for success that are shared with students before work or a task is assigned. This technique is familiar to many educators and is considered a formative assessment practice that increases the odds of student success.

Interestingly, establishing criteria for successful group interactions is often overlooked when working with adults. The assumption that most groups

**Table 5.4. Considerations for knowing when to integrate and when to insert oneself**

| Diagnosis | Intervention/action |
|---|---|
| Are group members clear about what is expected? (prework) | Criteria for success were developed prior to engaging in the work. |
| Does the group have the resourcefulness to figure out a path forward? | Do not intervene; expertise exists within the group. |
| Is the group unfamiliar with or has the group forgotten a specific practice? | Teach and/or model the practice or skill. |
| Can redirection be accomplished by asking a guiding question "outside" and not inserting oneself "inside" the group? | Redirect group to practice or skill. |
| First: Is this group likely to be unsuccessful without intervention? | Intervene for success of the group. |
| Second: What intervention is needed? | |
| Can data be gathered on how the intervention worked? | Assist groups with reflection for improvement next time. |

can figure it out is unrealistic because establishing a common understanding is necessary when colleagues with diverse views and opinions interact. Criteria for establishing successful group interactions can be described as follows:

- norms and working agreements are used;
- selected protocols and processes are in place for structure; and
- defined task completion or work products are clear.

Once criteria for successful group interactions are in place, diagnosis begins with assessing the best approach. Some actions that might be considered are the following: (1) do not intervene, (2) teach or model a skill or practice, (3) redirect group, (4) intervene with specific assistance, and (5) reflect on group processes and product for improvement. Table 5.4 is designed from the least to the most intrusive action and provides more detail than the aforementioned five considerations.

Knowing when and why to integrate or insert oneself into a group should always be guided by focusing on what is in the long-term best interest of the members of the group and the group as a whole. The view from the balcony is other-centered, and the desire to assert authority or demonstrate competence at the expense of group development diminishes one's influence with colleagues.

## CAPABILITY FOUR:
## USING INTERPERSONAL SKILLS TO CULTIVATE
## WORKING RELATIONSHIPS AND TO MOTIVATE
## AND MOBILIZE OTHERS (INDIVIDUALS AND GROUPS)

Cultivating working relationships begins with the ability to listen attentively to others without defensiveness. There is a lot at stake for a school leader in the day-to-day interactions with teachers. Teachers will decide to trust and engage in a process largely based on their perception of the leader's willingness to listen and accept feedback. Effective communication for school leaders includes

- listening to understand the thoughts, ideas, and concerns of others;
- presenting ideas and setting direction publicly; and
- influencing the way individuals and groups work and interact.

All three areas are essential for cultivating working relationships. (Listening to understand and influencing the way individuals work were already described in capability one.) This is because school leaders in the information age will need to distribute effective communication capabilities and practices to others.

The authors have observed that presenting ideas and managing conflict in public are two areas that are challenging for many principals. Principals have typically been teachers and are knowledgeable about how to present information to students. Anxiety seems to afflict many principals when a message needs to be presented to adults; the stakes are high, and the consequences if delivered poorly might be long term.

Three protocols designed to assist principals practice a message intended for presenting in public are the rehearsal, the pace and lead, and the challenging conversation protocols. (The protocols can also be used for an anticipated one-to-one conversation.) The three protocols offer an opportunity to focus and support a principal in delivering a practiced message.

The anxiety that speaking in public can cause is affirmed by the Statistic Brain Research Institute, which reports more people in the United States fear speaking in public (74 percent) than fear dying (68 percent; Statistic Brain Research Institute 2016). Rehearsing or practicing a conversation contributes to communicating a focused message, and the speaker is less prone to react to negative responses or conflict. Figure 5.1 is a rehearsal protocol that reduces anxiety because the speaker feels prepared and is less prone to lose focus while interacting with others.

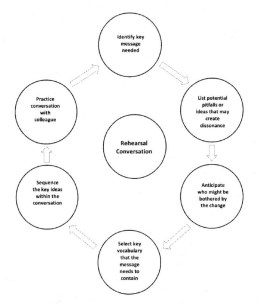

**Figure 5.1. Rehearsal conversation protocol**

A second area that challenges many principals, and they often report loss of sleep over this, is managing conflict, responding to defensiveness, and reframing unproductive conversations. There is no substitute for first establishing norms of collaboration and working agreements that describe how colleagues will engage one another privately and publicly. How a leader reacts or responds to conflict is informed by how conflict is understood and interpreted.

Reactions and responses to conflict should be informed by a broader view of human behavior and a decision to direct conflict into a cognitive rather than an emotional framework. Conflict is often interpreted as resistance to change, or an unwillingness to participate in new initiatives. Ronald Heifetz and Martin Linsky (2002) remind us that "people do not resist change, per se. People resist loss" (11). The sense of a temporary loss of identity, competence, or confidence is disorienting for many adults and can lead to unpredictable behaviors and internal conflict.

A school leader needs to model openness to ideas, calmness, confidence, and patience. It is particularly important for school leaders not to be defensive when others are passionate, confused, or angry. In the authors' work with school systems and schools, two types of responses to conflict. First, some leaders assert power and authority in ways that stifle discussion and conflict is not addressed, which influences unhealthy patterns of behavior. Second, some leaders avoid conflict, which can also stifle progress and influences unhealthy patterns of behavior.

Whether conflict is stifled or ignored, frustrations and disagreements can emerge as patterns of negative behaviors with conversation behind the scenes that is neither transparent nor positive. Cognitive conflict is inevitable and can be useful when addressed in an open and fair-minded manner.

## SUMMARY

School leaders are well served by being approachable and learning to listen to understand the thoughts, ideas, and concerns of others; present ideas and set direction publicly; and influence the way individuals and groups work and interact. These skills will lay the groundwork for cultivating working relationships with individuals and groups.

Ronald Riggio (2001) notes that "research has consistently shown that leaders who demonstrate consideration behaviors [leaders who are presumably more interpersonally sensitive] lead work groups who are more cohesive, more satisfied, and more productive. . . . Effective leadership is determined by the quality of the interaction between a leader and an individual work group member" (308). The disposition of communicating to influence provides the capabilities and practices for how to work with others effectively as seen through their eyes. It is with and through others that principals and teachers maintain a pervasive focus on student learning.

## MIDDLE SCHOOL VIGNETTE

Sunnydale Middle School has been working diligently to develop common practices that support student learning and set aside practices that do not meet agreed-upon instructional approaches. Through collaborative meetings, teachers are analyzing student work from common assessments and discussing structural and instructional supports that might better meet student needs.

Even with the concerted effort to focus on thinking and acting interdependently, the school leadership team noticed that the problem-solving processes were often stressful and limited in innovative thinking. It was felt that collective expertise was not being tapped in order to address complex situations.

Through observing at department collaboration, the leadership team noted that experienced staff members were speaking more frequently and putting more ideas on the table than were newer teachers. While still young in the profession, several of the new teachers entered into the job with high degrees of expertise. It was felt by the leadership team that it would be important to provide scaffolded opportunities to draw out the expertise from new teachers as well as from seasoned veterans.

To support the leadership team's effort, the principal decided it would be important to draw upon several resources that foster effective communication. She shared several protocols with the leadership team that were designed to foster opportunities to gather input from all participants in collaborative meetings. She also determined that during the next staff meeting she would share the kind of shifts she would like to see in the collaborative meetings so that deeper problem solving could take place. In order to be confident in her delivery of her message, the principal sketched, planned, and rehearsed the message with another principal in the district.

Her rehearsed message included the following:

## Acknowledgment of the Existing State

- acknowledgment of hard work being done within collaborative meetings
- understanding of the complexities of issues the staff is facing related to student needs
- appreciation for the efforts related to thinking and acting interdependently in recent months

## Description of the Desired State

- What we are going to do and why?
  - Increase the sharing of expertise from all members of the staff
  - Use a variety of processes and protocols to refine collaborative processes in order to foster deeper and more innovative problem-solving skills
- How we are going to do the work?
  - Use of dialogue prior to discussion when solving problems
  - Use of protocols in collaborative meetings to gather innovative thinking from all participants
  - Share leadership in facilitating the use of protocols
- When are we going to make the shift?
  - Beginning next month in department team meetings

The school principal drew upon the disposition of communicating to influence when she realized that valuable expertise was often absent in department meetings due to lack of sharing by newer, talented teachers. This type of thinking will assist her in creating a positive, trustworthy, and cognitively demanding environment where complex problem solving can take place. She considered the practices within the disposition and took action to put some of those practices into place with the staff.

## QUESTIONS TO ENGAGE YOUR THINKING AND DISCUSSION WITH COLLEAGUES

1. As you reflect on the collaborative meetings in your school, what practices within the disposition communicating to influence might be of assistance to you?
2. How might you consider organizing meetings to bring forth innovative thinking and complex problem solving from all staff members?

## REFERENCES

Dixon, N. (1998). *Dialogue at work: Making talk developmental for people and organizations*. London: Lemos & Crane.

Garmston, R., and Wellman, B. (2013). *The adaptive school: A sourcebook for developing collaborative groups*. Lanham, MD: Rowman & Littlefield.

Gordon, E. (Ed.). (2000). *Integrative neuroscience: Bringing together biological, psychological and clinical models of the human brain*. Singapore: Harwood Academic.

Heifetz, R. (1994). *Leadership without easy answers*. Cambridge, MA: Belknap Press of Harvard University Press.

Heifetz, R., and Linsky, M. (2002). *Leadership on the line: Staying alive through the dangers of leading*. Boston: Harvard Business School.

Leithwood, K. (2011). Leadership and student learning: What works and how. In J. Robertson and H. Timperley (Eds.), *Leadership and learning* (pp. 41–55). London: Sage.

Leithwood, K., and Seashore Louis, K. (2012). *Linking leadership to student learning*. San Francisco: Jossey-Bass.

Levitin, D. J. (2014). *The organized mind: Thinking straight in the age of information overload*. London: Penguin.

Medina, J. (2008). *Brain rules: 12 principles for surviving and thriving at work, home, and school*. Seattle: Pear Press.

Riggio, R. E. (2001). Interpersonal sensitivity research and organizational psychology: Theoretical and methodological applications. In J. Hall and F. Bernieri

(Eds.), *Interpersonal sensitivity: Theory and measurement* (pp. 305–318). Mahwah, NJ: Erlbaum.

Rock, D. (2009). *Your brain at work: Strategies for overcoming distraction, regaining focus, and working smarter all day long.* New York. HarperCollins.

Rock, D., and Cox, C. (2012). SCARF® in 2012: Updating the social neuroscience of collaborating with others. *NeuroLeadership Journal, 4.* Retrieved from https://neuroleadership.com/.

Statistic Brain Research Institute. (2016). Fear of public speaking statistics. Retrieved from http://www.statisticbrain.com/.

Weick, K. E. (1995). *Sensemaking in organizations.* Thousand Oaks, CA: Sage.

Weick, K. E., Sutcliffe, K. M., and Obstfeld, D. (2005). Organizing and the process of sensemaking. *Organization Science, 16*(4), 409–421.

Winnicott, D. W. (1960). The theory of the parent-infant relationship. *International Journal of Psychoanalysis, 41,* 585–595.

Woolley, A., Chabris, C., Pentland, A., Hashmi, N., and Malone, T. (2010). Evidence for a collective intelligence factor in the performance of human groups. *Science, 330*(6004), 686–688.

Woolley, A., and Malone, T. (2011). Defend your research: What makes a team smarter? More women. *Harvard Business Review, 89*(6), 32–33.

# 6

# GATHERING AND APPLYING INFORMATION FOR CHANGE

You must understand the whole of life, not just one little part of it.
That is why you must read, that is why you must look at the skies, that is
why you must sing and dance, and write poems, and suffer, and understand, for all that is life.

—J. Krishnamurti, Indian philosopher

In the current era of increased accountability, most school systems and schools are inundated with data. However, oftentimes these data are not systematically and intentionally gathered with the purpose of setting direction and informing change. In addition, too often individual prefer-ences and independent thinking compete with information gathered for evidence-based decision making.

In many of these instances, effective and efficacious decision making is thwarted even when data are systematically and intentionally gathered. For example, decision making may be based on individual preferences and subjective opinions rather than being grounded in the data that has been intentionally gathered. Other times, school systems and schools lack an environment that supports the type of inquiry needed to effectively gather and apply information for change.

Using data-based evidence to set direction and plan change requires an environment that regards educators as capable of using meaningful information. Within this type of environment educators utilize protocols and processes to discuss results and explore adjustments to programs and teaching. The dispositions of thinking and acting interdependently (see chapter 4) and communicating to influence (see chapter 5) are essential for developing this type of school environment that gathers and uses data to inform action and plan change.

The disposition of gathering and applying information for change directly addresses the problems often encountered in evidence-based decision making. In this book, the disposition *gathering and applying information for change* is defined as utilizing data-based evidence to make decisions and provide formative feedback for setting direction and planning change. This chapter explores the three capabilities of this disposition:

1. systematically and intentionally gathering and organizing needed data;
2. using data to inform actions; and
3. developing and nurturing an environment of inquiry and innovation grounded in reflection and continuous improvement.

This disposition intentionally frames *gathering and applying information* more broadly than the more commonly used term *data analysis* included in many school improvement approaches. School improvement approaches frequently focus on output measures and action plans based on the analyses of student test scores in content knowledge areas. However, absent from many of these action plans are meaningful opportunities to inquire systematically about the status of programs, curricula, and standards that are being implemented in a school.

In contrast, gathering and applying information in this disposition includes diverse types of data that go beyond academic measures, including both quantitative and qualitative sources of information for evidence-based decisions. In addition, this disposition includes the capabilities of *using data to inform actions and developing and nurturing an environment of inquiry and innovation* as essential components for ensuring that the gathered information is effectively used for continuous learning. Using data to inform actions addresses the challenge of idiosyncratic decisions and choices that are often made by principals and teachers working in isolation.

As noted in figure 6.1, the three capabilities for gathering and applying information for change are interconnected. Which data sources are used, how decisions are made, and the environment within a school or school system are as important as the information system itself that is designed to organize and disseminate data.

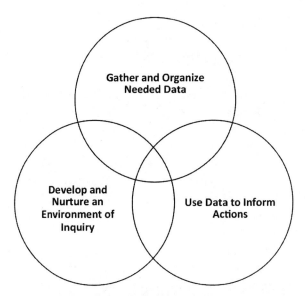

**Figure 6.I. Interconnected nature of gathering and applying information for continuous learning**

   Although each capability is described separately in this chapter, these three capabilities need to be interconnected and inseparably interdependent if a school system or school desires to focus on student learning and engage adults in continuous improvement. In addition, as described in more detail in this chapter, a principal who desires change based upon information about student learning must recognize that adult learning and development is central to an environment of inquiry and professional self-examination.

   The remainder of this chapter describes each of the three capabilities for the disposition of gathering and applying information for change: (1) systematically and intentionally gathering and organizing needed data; (2) using data to inform actions; and (3) developing and nurturing an environment of inquiry and innovation grounded in reflection and continuous improvement. Next, a middle school vignette is presented to contextualize the concepts in this chapter, followed by some questions to engage thinking and discussion with colleagues.

## CAPABILITY ONE: SYSTEMATICALLY AND INTENTIONALLY GATHERING AND ORGANIZING NEEDED DATA

The emphasis of many state departments of education and school districts, in response to accountability and school improvement, has been on analyzing and disseminating annual summative assessments aligned to state standards. The results from these measures of accountability are commonly and widely used by school systems and schools. Unfortunately, in many cases these large-scale summative assessments and their analyses have superseded the use of more practical and meaningful measurements that can inform teachers about improvement strategies or the influence on learning of specific instructional practices.

In addition, the heavy focus on accountability and school improvement has often undervalued and overlooked measures of metacognition, emotion, and motivation that are integral and equally as important to student learning as the acquisition of content knowledge. Given that student engagement in learning includes behavioral, emotional, and cognitive dimensions, setting direction and planning change should be based on data that is systematically and intentionally gathered about all these dimensions of student learning, rather than just academic content and achievement.

Therefore, this capability includes systematically and intentionally gathering and organizing needed data related to each of the following:

1. academic content and measures of schooling;
2. student engagement in the behavioral, emotional, and cognitive dimensions; and
3. information collected for evaluating implementation topics.

### Academic Content and Measures of Schooling

The most common focus area for systematically and intentionally gathering, organizing, and applying information involves data related to academic content and measures of schooling. The reauthorization of the Elementary and Secondary Education Act of 2002, known as No Child Left Behind (NCLB), focused the attention of the education community on the use of academic data. Subsequently, a significant amount of literature was generated addressing school improvement efforts that called for the collection, organization, and interpretation of data, as well as action planning based on academic data.

In addition to the focus on academic data spurred by NCLB, technology advancements in the twenty-first century also ushered in a "data-saturated" environment. And yet the plethora of technology-generated data is not always translated into an "information-rich" environment within schools and classrooms.

Information data systems are capable of efficiently disaggregating and displaying data at the district, school, classroom, and student levels. However, the human capacity to utilize the data generated by these information data systems often presents a significant challenge to schools and educators. A deluge of data and a lack of time to interpret the data often overwhelm educators.

In addition, the data collected and organized for school improvement typically result from large-scale summative assessments. These data are not generally associated with specific actions, and often the results aggregate both discrete learning targets and measurements across time. Subsequently, it is often difficult for teachers and principals to effectively use such measures for making small and meaningful adjustments to programs or instruction in real time.

Practical measurement addresses the capability of *gathering and organizing needed information* that is specific to an intended change and can be woven into the busy schedules of teachers and principals. Anthony Bryk (2015) observes that "introducing this kind of practical measurement poses a normative challenge as educators have traditionally seen data as intended for someone else—for a distant authority seeking to hold them accountable or a researcher studying them" (474). Teachers and principals need a sense of control about collecting relevant information that directly impacts teaching and learning.

In an agile organization, the school district shares the responsibility of designing and communicating a comprehensive data and information plan. The degree to which an entire organization activates the disposition of thinking and acting interdependently may well determine the effective uses of sources of information and data. A significant amount of confusion exists in a school system that cannot offer schools straightforward responses to how information and data are to be used.

Providing clarity about which data and information sources are used by whom and for what purposes appears to be a simple task. However, it is neither simple nor straightforward because many systems are overwhelmed by data and simply pass along the confusion to the school and classroom level. Table 6.1 outlines aspects of data and information literacy for asking

**Table 6.1.   Aspects of data and information literacy**

| Aspects of data and information literacy | Essential questions |
|---|---|
| System- and school-level requirements | Are data readily available and secure? Are web-based reporting systems readily accessible? |
| Types of data | What kinds of information are being collected, organized, and disseminated? |
| Uses of data | Are data analyzed for system and school accountability and improvement, as well as for student growth and learning? |
| Training and time | Are professional learning and adequate time established for interpreting information and tailored for how to apply insights and make needed changes? |
| Communication | Are interpersonal and group-process skills utilized to communicate data as formative feedback? |

and answering essential questions for designing a comprehensive data and information plan.

A major step for utilizing academic or content information effectively occurs when assessment inventories are developed, explained, and understood. For example, table 6.2 was designed as an inventory of diagnostic reading assessments for middle and high school. The assessment consists

**Table 6.2.   Example of diagnostic reading assessments (middle and high school)**

| Assessment | Purpose | Which students | Frequency |
|---|---|---|---|
| Globe Fearson's Secondary Reading Assessment Inventory (SRAI) | Assessing reading comprehension of secondary students | Students not meeting established targets | As needed to assess subskills |
| San Diego Quick Assessment of Reading | Recognition of words out of context for determining independent, instructional, and frustration levels | Students not meeting established targets for possible intervention | As needed to place student in an intervention program |
| Program Placement Assessments | Assessments are designed to place students in appropriate unit. | As needed to place students in specific level | As needed for placement |

of diagnostic tools. The inventory is designed to identify which assessments are used with students by stating the purpose and the frequency.

It is common for assessments to be misunderstood and misused when straightforward inventories are not used to provide guidance for principals and teachers. Similar inventories can be developed that denote local expectations, such as end-of-course tests, analytical writing assessments (AWA), performance-based assessments, or common assessments.

In the future, hopefully attention can be focused on adequately addressing practical measurement and formative assessment practices that provide educators and students with small and discrete amounts of feedback about acquisition of content knowledge. Many assessment inventories currently in place focus on reading and mathematics, core cognitive knowledge areas that are needed but also narrowly define learning.

Additionally, large-scale summative assessments are not designed to measure specific content delivered within a specific time frame. Designing assessments to be instructionally based and performance based will provide teachers and students with the feedback needed to closely link ideas taught and learned in a timely manner. These assessments should be used and reviewed throughout specific grade levels, or within departments, for systemically and intentionally making decisions.

## Student Engagement in the Behavioral, Emotional, and Cognitive Dimensions

A second focus area for gathering and applying data systematically involves first recognizing that emotion and motivation are integral aspects of learning. Student engagement, a term recognized by many researchers that encompasses aspects of metacognition, emotion, and motivation, is increasingly viewed as a critical component of student learning. In a review of the literature about student engagement, Jennifer Fredricks, Phyllis Blumenfeld, and Alison Paris (2004) suggest that it includes three dimensions of learning: behavioral, emotional, and cognitive. Engagement includes but is not limited to such important topics as persistence, belonging, and self-regulation.

A major challenge for school districts and schools is how to assess student engagement while honoring the idea that practical assessment must be easily embedded into a busy school calendar. Fredricks and colleagues (2011) reviewed twenty-one instruments that measure student engagement. The authors reported technical information on each instrument and list the dimensions and subscales of behavioral, emotional, and cognitive engagement.

It is important that each school district and school, in collaboration with their constituencies, defines student engagement and utilizes instruments that best assess their students.

Table 6.3 identifies important components of student engagement that educators might consider valuable when assessing the learning environment of a school. The self-reported student questions in the table are not field tested and are included only as examples. The examples would apply to upper elementary, middle school, and high school students.

**Table 6.3.  Aspects of student engagement for assessing the learning environment**

| Engagement dimension | Examples of self-reported questions |
| --- | --- |
| Behavioral persistence | If I don't understand something, I keep trying. |
| Behavioral engagement | I pay attention and focus on my teacher when asked. |
| Behavioral disaffection | I have given up trying in class. |
| Emotional belonging | School is a good place to be. |
| Emotional student-teacher relationships | Teachers care about my opinions and thoughts. |
| Emotional reaction to challenge | I like some schoolwork to be difficult. |
| Cognitive-strategy use reading | I look for signal words to help identify cause and effect when I read. |
| Cognitive planning | I plan the steps for writing a paper before I begin. |
| Cognitive study management | I usually study at home in a setting where I can concentrate. |

*Inspired by:* J. Fredricks, W. McColskey, J. Meli, J. Mordica, B. Montrosse, and K. Mooney (2011), *Measuring student engagement in upper elementary through high school: A description of 21 instruments*, Issues and Answers Report, REL 2011, No. 098 (Washington, DC: U.S. Department of Education, Institute of Education Sciences, National Center for Education Evaluation and Regional Assistance, Regional Educational Laboratory Southeast), retrieved from http://files.eric.ed.gov/.

The sample self-reported questions are the perceptions of students' experiences of school. It is important to consider the technical information about any instrument when measuring the behavioral, emotional, and cognitive dimensions of student engagement.

## Information Collected for Evaluating Implementation Topics

A third focus area for systematically and intentionally gathering and organizing information is designing a method for collecting and reviewing the status of implementation topics. Unfortunately, the perspective of the educators responsible for implementing new programs, new standards, or new curriculum is frequently overlooked. It is critical that schools establish feedback loops that include asking, receiving, and responding to how well an implementation is working from the point of view of teachers and other educators. Prior to assessing the progress of an implementation topic, three important features need to be in place:

1. an established building leadership team;
2. a two-way communication system for collecting information; and
3. knowledge of how to design high-quality invitational questions for eliciting the perspective of teachers.

A building leadership team that represents the departments or grade levels is used as a vehicle for two-way communication within a school. Schools are busy places and communication needs to be efficient and effective. A two-way system of communication between a principal and school staff is used for distributing and collecting important information. A principal works with a building leadership team to identify a school-wide implementation topic, and then collaboratively designs high-quality questions.

Asking high-quality questions and making adjustments based on the feedback is fundamental to setting the direction of a school. Table 6.4 identifies attributes of high-quality questions and a brief explanation of each. It is important to note that the way questions are asked reveals whether feedback is desired and if participation is genuinely encouraged. High-quality questions that encourage reflection and creativity are nondichotomous, open ended, and invitational in nature. High-quality questions also contain plural forms and tentative language to communicate that feedback is encouraged and desired.

An effective and simple method for obtaining feedback from teachers is when a principal and a building leadership team develop and distribute one question every two weeks or so. Requesting feedback in a busy school

**Table 6.4.   Attributes of high-quality questions**

| Attribute | Explanation |
| --- | --- |
| Nondichotomous | Encourages responses that are not yes/no or true/false |
| Open ended | Allows responses that are not limited or directive |
| Invitational | Communicates tone that is friendly and genuine |
| Plural forms | Communicates that more than one way is possible |
| Tentative language | Utilizes words such as might, could, and possibly |

Source: A. Costa and R. Garmston (2015), *Cognitive coaching: Developing self-directed leaders and learners* (3rd Ed.) (Lanham, MD: Rowman & Littlefield).

feels more manageable when one thoughtfully written question is distributed to the school staff at infrequent intervals. For example, a grade-level or department meets to discuss and craft a statement to a question; then a response that reflects the thoughts of the entire team is submitted to the principal and building leadership team.

There are two purposes for having a grade-level or department team develop a response as an initial step. First, the team members have the opportunity to hear the viewpoint or ideas of their colleagues and develop a greater understanding of different perspectives. Second, the amount of feedback that needs to be processed by the principal and leadership team is reduced when grade-level teams or departments formulate a group response. Textbox 6.1 presents sample high-quality questions.

---

**Textbox 6.1. Sample high-quality questions**

What are some of the celebrations with the new implementation?

What might be some of the most challenging aspects of this implementation?

What might you consider if you were to redesign the writing program using evidence-based practices?

What information might be helpful as we modify or adjust this . . . ?

How might we improve the quality of behavior data collected?

In what areas might we need additional support to improve this implementation?

What have been the top two to three reasons this implementation has been so successful?

What modules/units/themes from the reading/math materials have been covered in your classroom thus far? (pacing)

---

The sample questions in textbox 6.1 include the elements of high-quality questions noted in table 6.4. The last question in the table is not open ended or tentative when compared to the other questions in the table. This question would be used for generating specific information about the status of program pacing or curricula by a specific group of teachers.

There are times when questions need to be asked that do not contain all attributes of high-quality questions. However, an invitational tone should always be used when eliciting feedback from colleagues. It is important to state, in advance, how high-quality questions will be processed and whether the faculty will be having a dialogue or discussion about a topic.

## CAPABILITY TWO: USING DATA TO INFORM ACTIONS

Establishing routines that support the collection, analysis, and use of both quantitative and qualitative data for making decisions, setting direction, and planning change creates a sense of predictability and certainty with the technical aspects of using information. In addition, as explored in the discussion of the disposition communicating to influence (see chapter 5), effective decisions are made by utilizing inclusive group processes. When protocols are routinely utilized, educators focus on data-informed strategies and solutions that assist with improving student learning.

For example, a principal can work collaboratively with the building leadership team to leverage the capability of using data to inform actions by developing and implementing a calendar that notes the types of data that will be analyzed and discussed. Table 6.5 presents a sample cycle-of-work calendar that establishes a predictable routine for a building leadership team. This calendar includes overall assessments topics that were in place on the initial calendar, as well as specific details for questions about implementation topics that were developed one month at a time.

Content, program, or academic data analyses should be considered as a yearlong cycle with patterns and rhythms to the work. Data should be analyzed as soon as possible after the administration of an assessment and noted on a cycle-of-work calendar. For example, universal screening data is generally best utilized during the fall, winter, and spring time frames within the year.

The role of the building leadership team is to review school-wide, grade-level, or department-level data. The building leadership team does not review individual student-level data. The building leadership team's role for data analyses is to look for patterns of performance, suggest options for organizing school resources, and examine school schedules for student placement.

A cycle-of-work calendar should also include an opportunity for the building leadership team to assess its own effectiveness. Questions for team reflection can focus on the assessment system, core instruction, and practices for data analyses. The questions should be crafted and distributed before meetings to provide clarity of purpose and predictability about the actions needed by the team. For example, the questions noted in tables 6.6 and 6.7 are examples of questions that could be asked during the final quarter of a school year. The sample questions in table 6.6 focus on the assessment system and core instruction.

**Table 6.5.  Sample cycle-of-work calendar for a building leadership team**

| Month | Initial agenda topics and data sources |
|---|---|
| September: first meeting | Review working agreement; identify facilitators, agenda format, and bank of protocols. Distribute team message about universal screening assessment dates in reading and math and clarification about new writing program to the staff. |
| September: second meeting | Review universal screening data using standard protocol model; assess student placement in interventions based on data. Develop high-quality question about pacing of the new writing program. |
| October: first meeting | Process response from high-quality question about writing program and craft feedback to staff. Distribute message about progress monitoring data in reading and math. Distribute message about student engagement use of cognitive strategies survey in reading. |
| October: second meeting | Review progress monitoring data and assess student placement based on data. Review student responses to using cognitive strategies in reading and distribute results to staff. Develop high-quality question for teachers' thoughts about students' responses to cognitive strategies' survey in reading. |
| November: first meeting | Process response from high-quality question about cognitive strategies' survey in reading and craft feedback to the staff. Use problem-solving protocol to review challenges from informal feedback about the writing program implementation (e.g., appears more teacher training is needed and a faculty-wide *dialogue* about pacing might be needed). |
| November: second meeting | Develop a process for faculty *dialogue* about writing program for school-wide faculty meeting. Develop high-quality questions and briefly rehearse roles of building leadership team members at the meeting. Review the use of diagnostic assessments in reading from faculty self-report. Craft a response to faculty and clarify use of diagnostic assessments in reading. |

The sample questions in table 6.7 focus on data analyses and the effectiveness of the building leadership team. A building leadership team that reflects on their experiences provides a model for how a grade-level or department-level team might examine their own teamwork. A well-functioning building leadership team is integral for analyzing diverse and comprehensive forms of data, establishing a two-way system of communication, and setting direction and planning change.

**Table 6.6.   Sample assessment system and core instruction questions**

| Assessment system questions | Core instruction questions |
|---|---|
| What might need adjusting with our universal screening system to improve it for next year? | What do the spring data say about improved student learning with our focus areas in core instruction? |
| What might need adjusting with our early warning system to improve it for next year? | What adjustments might need to be made for next year in order to support strong core instruction? |
| Will we be using any new measures in our assessment system that need implementation planning (state-level summative assessments, progress monitoring, and program assessments)? | Based on the spring screening data, which grades/departments might need additional support next year? |
| To what degree was the assessment system used to make decisions regarding student learning? | Based on spring results, what professional development needs do we have for fall and the next year with academics and behavior? |

The capability of using data to inform actions such as making decisions, setting direction, and planning change requires that needed information is being systematically and intentionally gathered and organized by the principal and building leadership team. As discussed in the previous capability, these needed data include academic content measures, student engagement measures, and high-quality questions about implementation topics.

**Table 6.7.   Sample data analyses and building leadership team questions**

| Data analyses questions | Building leadership team questions |
|---|---|
| How might we improve the way we organize data so that it is efficient and effective in analyzing data for examining growth? | How effective were we with meeting consistently for our work? |
| What adjustments might need to be made regarding data-analysis processes for building leadership team meetings? | What adjustments might we need to make to our working agreement for the year? |
| What adjustments might need to be made regarding processes and protocols for analyzing data for next year? | What further clarity do we need to refine our roles and responsibilities for next year? |
| What additional knowledge/skill will the staff need next year regarding instructional and structural adjustments that might need to be made after data are analyzed? | What might need to be improved with our two-way communication system for next year? |

## CAPABILITY THREE: DEVELOPING AND NURTURING AN ENVIRONMENT OF INQUIRY AND INNOVATION GROUNDED IN REFLECTION AND CONTINUOUS IMPROVEMENT

Effectively using data-based evidence to make decisions requires a school environment that supports and values inquiry, innovation, reflection, and continuous improvement. Systematically collecting and using information for setting the direction of a school will not happen in the absence of this type of school environment. Developing and nurturing this type of environment of inquiry and innovation grounded in reflection and continuous improvement is first and foremost about embedding principles of adult learning and development within the school environment.

Supporting and nurturing adult learning and development, as described by Eleanor Drago-Severson (2009), requires essential features such as the following:

- focusing on posing questions,
- providing resources of time and expertise,
- utilizing relevant data,
- using protocols for analyzing data and discussing it, and
- defining roles team members might assume.

Textbox 6.2 lists essential features for creating the conditions whereby professionals are willing to examine their practices in an environment

### Textbox 6.2. Nurturing adult development

**Essential Features for Nurturing Adult Development**

Focusing on question posing instead of question answering
Providing resources such as time, data, and expertise for teams to collaborate effectively
Providing adults with relevant data to analyze
Providing teachers with tools for accessing useable data and protocols for analyzing and discussing it
Considering membership (composition of the team) and the roles members might assume

*Source:* E. Drago-Severson (2009), *Leading adult learning: Supporting adult development in our schools* (Thousand Oaks, CA: Corwin).

where being *curious about* results replaces assigning *blame for* results. This capability also requires applying practices from the dispositions of thinking and acting interdependently (see chapter 4) and communicating to influence (see chapter 5).

The structures that nurture adult development with a pervasive focus on student learning contribute to an environment where educators are accountable to students and to one another. The disposition of gathering and applying information for change related to organizational improvement can ensure that the system is continually evaluating, and attending to, routines and practices that may impede learning.

Correspondingly, using multiple forms of data can serve as a guide for inquiry to determine whether or not current practices are effective. Alexander Platt and colleagues (2008) emphasize that lack of effective data use undermines learning. As noted in textbox 6.3, the authors describe inefficient or unpromising practices for using data that should be avoided or addressed when establishing a data use system. The authors note that use of evidence-based decision making is necessary for setting organizational direction and planning change that supports improved student learning.

---

### Textbox 6.3. Unpromising practices for using data

**Six Unpromising Practices**

Strict adherence to standard operating procedures and business as usual without evidence that those procedures actually improve student learning

Substituting attention to actions for attention to outcomes

Willful, persistent disregard of the effects of actions and decisions on learners

A habit of focusing blame, explanations, and solution-finding almost exclusively on external factors

Large, random expenditures of effort (and sometimes funds) on activities and initiatives that are not clearly linked to data-driven learning goals or learning needs

Inability or unwillingness to ask hard questions about your own practice or resorting to "edubabble" in response to hard questions

*Source:* A. D. Platt, C. E. Tripp, R. G. Fraser, J. R. Warnock, and R. E. Curtis (2008), *The skillful leader II: Confronting conditions that undermine learning* (Acton, MA: Ready About Press).

One approach for addressing unpromising practices is structuring dialogue based on the essential features that nurture adult development (see textbox 6.4). For example, Drago-Severson (2009) asserts that focusing on question posing rather than question answering is a starting point. Textbox 6.4 provides examples of questions that may be posed to support or guide inquiry through adult development. These questions alert participants before convening that dialogue will be solution oriented, be focused on student learning, and rely on how participants might change their own practices based on information.

## Textbox 6.4. High-quality questions to guide inquiry

### Questions that Support Inquiry through Adult Development

Which data would serve us best for this inquiry?
After reviewing the data, which instructional routines and procedures do we currently use that might need to be adjusted?
Considering the student engagement data, which of our own practices might we adjust to increase engagement of our students?
What protocols and processes are currently in place to assist us with effective, accurate, and solution-based analyses?
To what degree have we developed distributed leadership capabilities for collecting, displaying, and analyzing data to support improved student learning?

Insights are developed within an environment that values creativity, and these insights can only happen when thinking is invited by first asking high-quality questions rather than asserting opinions or answers. The benefits of asking well-crafted, high-quality questions include the following:

- builds a common understanding,
- strengthens shared ideas,
- assists in gaining multiple perspectives, and
- challenges assumptions.

One of the best possible outcomes from asking well-crafted high-quality questions is gaining insights into how challenges might be addressed and solved. Abraham Joshua Heschel (1969) suggests that an insight is "the perception of things to come rather than an extension of things gone by" (3).

## SUMMARY

Successful leaders are in a continuous learning mode regarding student learning and implementations within their school. Their confidence, in combination with their curiosity, allows them to constantly search for new and better ways for their organization to learn and improve. They gather needed data to inform their decisions and actions, set direction, and plan change. They develop and nurture an environment of inquiry and innovation grounded in reflection and continuous improvement.

For example, a principal who desires change based upon information about student learning must recognize that adult learning and development is central to an environment of inquiry and professional self-examination. The disposition of gathering and applying information for change includes establishing processes and protocols for collecting and examining both quantitative and qualitative data. The purpose of establishing these mechanisms is to closely investigate current levels of student learning and engagement, as well as the current status of implementation within the school.

## MIDDLE SCHOOL VIGNETTE

The Sunnydale Middle School staff has a long, successful history of analyzing quantitative data at both the school and the department level. Delissa has been the principal for the last four years. The staff is facile with data to make adjustments for instructional groups and individual students. As new teachers join the staff at Sunnydale, time is spent in department meetings discussing the assessment system and quantitative data displays, as well as potential instructional implications based on the data.

A school leadership team has been formed to support school-wide implementations designed to improve student learning. The leadership team meets once a month with team membership comprising department heads, a special education teacher, a counselor, and the school principal. While the school has received extensive professional development with analyzing and using quantitative data, facility with understanding and using data related to school-wide implementations is new work.

Delissa recognized that the school leadership team would benefit from the opportunity to develop protocols and processes for collecting, interpreting, sharing, and problem solving with qualitative data related to an implementation. One major area of collecting qualitative data that warranted team collaboration was that of crafting high-quality questions. Delissa and the leadership team decided to use the attributes of high-quality questions (see table 6.4) as a resource for developing questions.

The leadership team identified the school-wide implementation of *using text structure with informational text* for their use of collecting qualitative data. In order to create two-way communication with all teachers, the team crafted a high-quality question at the end of each meeting. The question is shared at each department team meeting, and a leadership team member, trained in the use of dialogue, provides an opportunity for feedback. The leadership team member organizes a summary of responses related to the implementation question.

The feedback from each department is shared at the beginning of each leadership team meeting. The leadership uses protocols such as traffic lighting, chalk talk, or 3-2-1 to identify themes from the responses. Delissa decided not to facilitate the reporting out of themes and only asks clarifying questions when she is unsure of something.

Delissa and the school leadership team had a better understanding about the *implementation of using text structure with informational text* by asking teachers high-quality questions. The feedback from departments led to both offering professional-learning opportunities and modeling and observing the use of *text structure with informational text* in classrooms. Delissa, the leadership team, and the majority of teachers at Sunnydale Middle School decided using qualitative data to improve an implementation was worth the investment of their time.

## QUESTIONS TO ENGAGE YOUR THINKING AND DISCUSSION WITH COLLEAGUES

1. What are some opportunities for you to consider regarding refining ways of collecting, analyzing, and using quantitative and qualitative information?
2. What qualitative information may be of assistance to you regarding an implementation in your school?
3. How might the leadership team in your school be of assistance with designing high-quality questions, collecting, analyzing, and using qualitative information?

## REFERENCES

Boudett, K., City, E., and Murnane, R. (2013). *Data wise: A step-by-step guide to using assessment results to improve teaching and learning.* Cambridge, MA: Harvard Education Press.

Bryk, A. (2015, December). Accelerating how we learn to improve. *Educational Researcher, 44*(89), 467–477.

Costa, A., and Garmston, R. (2015). *Cognitive coaching: Developing self-directed leaders and learners* (3rd Ed.). Lanham, MD: Rowman & Littlefield.

Drago-Severson, E. (2009). *Leading adult learning: Supporting adult development in our schools.* Thousand Oaks, CA: Corwin.

Fredricks, J. A., Blumenfeld, P. C., and Paris, A. (2004). School engagement: Potential of the concept: State of the evidence. *Review of Educational Research, 74*, 59–119.

Fredricks, J., McColskey, W., Meli, J., Mordica, J., Montrosse, B., and Mooney, K. (2011). *Measuring student engagement in upper elementary through high school: A description of 21 instruments.* Issues and Answers Report, REL 2011, No. 098. Washington, DC: U.S. Department of Education, Institute of Education Sciences, National Center for Education Evaluation and Regional Assistance, Regional Educational Laboratory Southeast. Retrieved from http://files.eric.ed.gov/.

Heschel, A. J. (1969). *The prophets.* New York: Harper Row.

Platt, A. D., Tripp, C. E., Fraser, R. G., Warnock, J. R., and Curtis, R. E. (2008). *The skillful leader II: Confronting conditions that undermine learning.* Acton, MA: Ready About Press.

## 7

# SEEKING SUPPORT
# AND FEEDBACK FOR LEARNING

A person and an organization must have goals, take actions to achieve those goals, gather evidence of achievement, study and reflect on the data and from that take actions again. Thus, they are in a continuous feedback spiral toward continuous improvement. This is what "Kaizan" means.

—W. Edwards Deming

Leadership has an intrapersonal dimension, a knowledge and understanding of self, that is integral to resiliency and professional growth as a leader. The intrapersonal dimensions for a leader include an understanding and willingness to develop or enhance self-knowledge, self-awareness, and self-efficacy. Self-knowledge, self-awareness, and self-efficacy are equally necessary attributes to ensure that leaders are conscious of their leadership influence, are capable of introspection, and can withstand criticism and difficult feedback.

Humility is also a needed quality so leaders might learn from others and from their mistakes in order to recognize areas for growth from feedback. Humility is the leavening agent needed so a leader's intrapersonal growth is used to focus efforts not on elevating the self but rather on adult and student learning and development. Gordon Donaldson (2008) contends that intrapersonal learning requires looking inward and honestly asking oneself where one needs to grow and improve as a leader. It is hard work to assess one's strengths and weaknesses in order to strive to be an impactful leader.

This chapter explores the disposition of *seeking support and feedback for learning* that increases resiliency and fosters professional growth toward excellence. The four capabilities of this disposition that are discussed in this chapter are follows:

1. developing self-knowledge, self-awareness, and self-efficacy while maintaining a sense of humility;
2. frequently seeking feedback focused on learning and professional growth;
3. engaging in a collegial network of high-performing teams of principals; and
4. creating feedback spirals for continuous individual and organizational self-learning.

In addition, this chapter provides a middle school vignette to contextualize this disposition and its capabilities, and provides questions to engage the readers' thinking and discussion with colleagues.

## CAPABILITY ONE: DEVELOPING SELF-KNOWLEDGE, SELF-AWARENESS, AND SELF-EFFICACY WHILE MAINTAINING A SENSE OF HUMILITY

The disposition of seeking support and feedback for learning recognizes that the growth of principals begins with the intrapersonal areas of self-knowledge, self-awareness, and self-efficacy. Personal growth and professional excellence are interconnected and must be addressed simultaneously. The self-schema is multifaceted and can be approached from different perspectives depending upon the intent for examining oneself.

The self-schema of knowledge, awareness, and efficacy will be used in this chapter because it describes the intrapersonal dimension for developing and maturing as a school leader. Table 7.1 summarizes these powerful intrapersonal dimensions of leadership that can be considered the understanding of self, or intrapersonal literacy. Interpersonal literacy, in the context of leadership, affirms the development of knowledge, awareness, and efficacy to influence and inspire others.

*Self-knowledge* is having an understanding of the mental models and values that one uniquely pairs with oneself. Self-knowledge is knowing one's strengths and weaknesses, one's beliefs and biases, and the values that motivate one's decisions. For example, Viviane Robinson (2011) contends

**Table 7.1.   Intrapersonal dimensions of leadership**

| | |
|---|---|
| Self-knowledge | Understanding the mental models and values that one uniquely pairs with oneself |
| Self-awareness | Capacity for introspection in order to compare one's behavior with internal mental models or values while making needed adjustments |
| Self-efficacy | Capacity to exercise self-influence and a belief in one's ability to succeed |

that effective school leaders are motivated by a pervasive focus on student learning and providing a high-quality learning environment for all students.

*Self-awareness* is the capacity for introspection and the ability to compare one's behavior to internal mental models or values. Self-awareness leads to viewing behavior in the context of its impact on others while making needed adjustments. It allows leaders to appreciate other people and gain insight into how they might be perceived. Self-awareness inspires educators to reflect on one's actions to see if they are congruent with one's espoused beliefs. For instance, leaders might want to make reasoned and sound decisions, and yet discover through experience that their impulsive responses have often led to poor decisions.

*Self-efficacy* is the capacity to exercise self-influence and a belief in one's ability to succeed. It allows an individual to move forward in the face of criticism, ambiguity, uncertainty, or unpopular decisions. Self-efficacy is the belief that tasks can be completed and goals can be reached. A strong sense of self-efficacy sustains leaders in the face of criticism so they might interpret an experience as an opportunity to learn and adjust rather than as a failure or setback.

For example, the initial attempt to implement new materials combined with new instructional strategies may lead to teacher frustration and criticism. The principal with a strong sense of self-efficacy, who can think flexibly based on critical feedback to ensure a smoother transition, will be able to view the experience as growth rather than a setback.

Table 7.2 provides examples of each of these intrapersonal dimensions. The journey toward intrapersonal development is never-ending. However, the examples of intrapersonal literacy in this table invite readers to assess themselves at this point in time and in the spirit of humility.

An understanding and balance of these intrapersonal dimensions of self-knowledge, self-awareness, and self-efficacy is essential for school leaders because their professional lives are public—in a sense on display—for teachers, students, and parents to observe and critique. Understanding

**Table 7.2. Examples of the intrapersonal dimensions**

| | |
|---|---|
| Self-knowledge | I have a solid understanding of my *personal* strengths and weaknesses. |
| | I have a solid understanding of my *professional* strengths and weaknesses. |
| | I have a strong understanding of what motivates me and makes me happy *personally*. |
| | I have a strong understanding of what motivates me and makes me happy *professionally*. |
| | I am aware of the beliefs and values that guide my work as a leader. |
| Self-awareness | I delay forming premature conclusions and can manage the impulse to take immediate action. |
| | I have established conscious metacognitive strategies to monitor the effectiveness of my plans and to help me make any necessary alterations. |
| | I have an understanding that a sense of humility is needed in order to learn from others. |
| Self-efficacy | I persevere when criticized for generating alternative plans of action. |
| | I recover quickly when difficult experiences cause me to evaluate, analyze, and construct meaning in order to change myself. |
| | I am curious and self-motivated, and view continuous learning as an opportunity rather than something to be avoided. |
| | I gather formative feedback (formally or informally) from others in order to grow as a leader, even when feedback is critical. |
| | I am open and willing to relinquish certain ideas in favor of other, more valid ones and do not view making adjustments as a personal or professional setback. |

and balancing these intrapersonal dimensions, in turn, requires a sense of humility.

A sense of humility about oneself, knowing that one may not know everything, is one of the highest forms of thinking we can ever learn. A sense of humility allows school leaders to communicate what they may not know, that they are receptive to other viewpoints and opinions, and are willing to learn from mistakes and criticism. Prime and Salib (2014) discovered in their research about inclusive leadership practices that humility played an important role in influencing participation of group members and modeled the desire to learn from others.

One great mystery about humans is that learning opportunities are often greeted with fear rather than curiosity and wonder. Individuals seem to feel better when they know, rather than when they learn. Defending one's biases, beliefs, and storehouses of knowledge is the more common stance rather than inviting the unknown, the creative, and the inspirational.

The notion that the heroic school leader should always have the answers is unrealistic and reinforces the desire to defend and justify decisions.

School leaders benefit from being in continuous learning mode. Self-efficacy, in combination with inquisitiveness, allows for a constant search for new and better ways, while acknowledging that problems and conflicts are valuable opportunities to learn. Humility allows individuals to value moments of doubt and explore alternatives rather than provide quick answers. Self-efficacy allows individuals to take action and make adjustments when tasks are difficult or goals require persistence.

Contemporary educational environments will demand an environment that fosters people who are eager to learn. Paradoxically, the attributes and skills leaders possess that demonstrate control and competence might not be considered helpful by others, unless leaders begin by modeling humility. School leaders should realize that no one is perfect and that strong and effective school leaders do not try to pretend that they are perfect.

## CAPABILITY TWO: FREQUENTLY SEEKING FEEDBACK FOCUSED ON LEARNING AND PROFESSIONAL GROWTH

Efficacious school leaders, considering the examples of intrapersonal literacy in table 7.2, will see themselves as a learner among learners. Inspired by utilizing the intrapersonal dimensions of leadership, these school leaders will continually seek to strengthen shortcomings rather than cover them up. Humility will compel these leaders to display patience with others' weaknesses while realizing that influence and inspiration are more helpful than criticism. These leaders will regularly ask themselves such role identity questions as:

- What have I learned about my role as school leader?
- Who am I becoming?
- Whom do I want to become?
- How are others perceiving me as a result of my interactions with them over time?

To find support for themselves as learners, effective leaders actively and frequently seek feedback and continually assess themselves to determine when they may need to pursue a new set of skills. Believing in their own ability to learn about a wide range of topics, efficacious leaders set professional growth goals for themselves. As they gain insights from research and evidence for their own experiences, they deliberately apply those insights and practice those skills to become the best that they can be.

Therefore, the second capability within this disposition is frequently seeking feedback from teachers, colleagues, and supervisors for the purposes of learning and professional growth. Although feedback is a topic mentioned frequently in the education literature, much of this research, such as that by John Hattie (2009) and Dylan Wiliam (2011), focuses on feedback provided to students.

Feedback for adults is less represented in the education literature, and given the recent national focus on employee evaluation systems, feedback for educators is often designed for accountability purposes rather than focusing on learning and professional growth. Feedback in an evaluative setting provides a rating, but it may or may not lead to growth and learning.

Therefore, an important consideration within this capability is the notion that not all feedback is of equal value or has a positive impact. Avraham Kluger and Angelo DeNisi (1996) conducted a comprehensive meta-analysis for developing a theory of feedback intervention. The meta-analysis indicated that feedback was only helpful about one-third of the time due to common mistakes made by those poorly trained or those with negative intentions. Their findings are instructive for using feedback as a tool for improving the job performance of adults. These findings include the following:

- The focus of feedback needs to be limited and reasonably simple.
- Feedback about the nature of the task or action that is novel or complex is less likely to be understood.
- When feedback is about the self (person), and not the task or data, it will be interpreted ambivalently or negatively.
- The cues (body language, voice tone, and language use) from the message exhibited by the giver of feedback will be interpreted as positive or negative, influencing whether the information is well received.
- The self-efficacy, self-esteem, and locus of control of the person receiving feedback will influence whether the feedback is processed or helpful.
- Feedback that criticizes, threatens self-esteem, demeans the intellect, and raises concerns about career can actually be harmful.

Other research also notes the shortcomings of traditional performance feedback systems, finding that improved performance is an outcome only if learning and growth are the focus of feedback. For example, Steven Scullen, Michael Mount, and Maynard Goff (2000) determined in their research of performance ratings that over half of the variance of ratings was due to "idiosyncratic rater effects." In other words, the ratings revealed more about the rater than the person being rated.

These shortcomings of performance feedback systems are being recognized by many private-sector companies who are abandoning annual performance reviews, including Microsoft, Adobe, Dell, Accenture, New York Life, and Deloitte. The change in direction is due to

- low employee engagement in the performance review process;
- lack of influence of current reviews to improve performance;
- significant amount of time spent on the current performance review process; and
- anxiety of the managers delivering, and the employees receiving, performance reviews.

Given these shortcomings, performance review systems are being replaced by more frequent feedback that is lower stakes and replaces the more traditional once-a-year high-stakes review. Additionally, self-assessments are increasingly being used to focus on building assets rather than highlighting deficits. The point of changing the performance review system is to engage in ongoing and frequent conversations with both colleagues and supervisors. Feedback needs to be specific, manageable, factual, alterable, and professional to encourage learning and growth as indicated in table 7.3.

**Table 7.3.    Attributes of feedback for adult learning and growth**

| | |
|---|---|
| Specific | Feedback has to be about the task, process, or activity. Data or information needs to be tangible and clear and cannot be implied, vague, or general. |
| Manageable | Feedback needs to be simple. Complex or novel topics need to be simplified as much as possible. Cognitive load—the amount of information being processed—has to be monitored. Feedback communicated with greater frequency simplifies the process. |
| Factual | Data and agreed-upon factual information (goal setting or self-assessments) lead to transparency of the feedback. Opinions and criticism negatively impact a feedback relationship. The "self or person" is not the focus of feedback. (The three-point technique is utilized.) |
| Alterable | Behaviors, not personal characteristics, can be changed and adjusted. Recipients of feedback need a sense of the locus of control and a degree of positive self-efficacy so feedback can influence change. |
| Professional | Effective interpersonal skills, such as voice tone, body language, pausing, paraphrasing, and posing effective questions, must be used. Engage in a collaborative, not an imposed, process. |

Feedback meeting these characteristics outlined in table 7.3 is essential for learning and professional growth. The demands of leading a school as a public figure provide opportunities to receive both positive and negative feedback from teachers, parents, community members, and immediate supervisors. Feedback can be useful, but it can also be critical, harmful, or even undeserved.

Two important aspects of the type of feedback noted in this capability are that (1) the feedback is actively solicited by the school leader, and (2) the feedback is explicitly for the purposes of learning and professional growth. Frequent feedback actively sought in this type of collegial setting needs to be informative and be designed with growth as the outcome, so that principals can strive to lead brilliantly.

Feedback in a collegial setting is a mutual decision made by colleagues and is used to provide support in areas such as honing a leader's interpersonal communication skills of listening, pausing, paraphrasing, and posing well-crafted questions. Learning for growth requires feedback that is nonjudgmental, communicated professionally, and intended to support and assist the recipient. Principals who can model how to receive and provide informative feedback have a vehicle for positively impacting the culture of their respective schools.

Grade-level, department-level, or any learning community configuration within a school creates an opportunity for predictable routines for seeking and processing feedback. For feedback to become the fabric of a leadership culture, it should not be considered occasional or idiosyncratic. A commitment to regularly soliciting informative feedback in this environment is represented by the saying, "It is better to receive than to give."

## CAPABILITY THREE: ENGAGING IN A COLLEGIAL NETWORK OF HIGH-PERFORMING TEAMS OF PRINCIPALS

Principals begin the path to excellence and growth by exhibiting humility, recognizing they might not know how to proceed, and being unafraid to find out (Costa 2001). A critical ingredient for ongoing support and growth is participation in a collegial network to enhance efficacy and resiliency. Whereas the previous capability is focused on the more immediate, and less formal, systems of feedback for learning and growth, this capability focuses on the principal's more formal participation in a collegial network focused on long-term learning goals and professional growth.

A collegial network, or networked leadership community, is designed to use high-performing teams of principals to increase informative feedback, provide encouragement and support, and increase the translation of goal setting to action that improves student learning. Members of a networked leadership community recognize that success as a principal in a professional setting (the public self) is accomplished by the development of the self-efficacy needed to grow, learn, and persist as an individual.

The historical notion of the heroic leader leading by individual effort, isolated and standing apart from others, is not sustainable and often leads to disillusionment and job burnout. According to the Hechinger Report (Tyre 2015), more than half of principals quit within five years of taking a position, and data reported by the School Leaders Network (2014) note that 50 percent of new principals quit during their third year in the role. Similarly, a MetLife survey (Markow, Macia, and Lee 2012) reports that about one-third of principals report they are very or fairly likely to leave their job and actually seek employment in a different profession.

Principals acknowledge their role as school leader has become more complex, while experiencing frequent job-related stress and high levels of burnout. Networks of support are even more critical given that the confidential nature of many situations in the principalship often leads to isolation. Fatih Ozbay and colleagues (2007) carefully reviewed the research literature related to stress, isolation, and resilience. The authors concluded that having access to robust social networks actually has "protective effects" for maintaining both physical and psychological health.

Therefore, leaders in high-stress environments with the potential for job burnout need these collegial networks to provide support and feedback, enhance resiliency, and reduce stress. Robert Waldinger (2015) draws three significant conclusions from the Harvard Study of Adult Development:

- healthy social connections sustain us;
- the quality of close relationships matter; and
- good relationships protect our health.

This longitudinal study focused on personal relationships, but the same conclusions apply to professional lives. For example, an intentional process for developing supportive relationships for health-care professionals called the Schwartz Center Rounds has been found to reduce isolation, burnout, and stress for participants.

School leaders work daily in an environment where there is an absence of others who are in the same role with similar responsibilities. The structure of a school setting does not naturally afford opportunities for peer support and encouragement for a school principal. Thus, those opportunities must be intentionally pursued, socially constructed, and fostered with other school leaders. A system of support and a collegial network for principals can

- provide encouragement, support, and feedback;
- foster resilience; and
- reduce a sense of isolation.

School leaders need collegial networks to enhance their personal and professional growth. Professional learning communities and communities of practice have become commonplace in education, particularly for teachers. However, networked leadership communities are less common for school leaders. Networked leadership communities that focus on the self-efficacy of individual principals, as well as on sharing expertise for how to implement changes to improve student learning, are virtually nonexistent.

## Problems of Practice versus Practice-Based Evidence

Historically, school leadership efforts to improve student learning ignored the need to simultaneously focus on the capabilities of the principal leading the effort. Focusing solely on the technical aspect of implementing changes made it easier to isolate barriers and problems ascribed to the fidelity of implementing evidence-based practices. This is referred to as the "problems of practice." Problems of practice are actually the challenges encountered by the complexity associated with implementing research-based practices in diverse circumstances, with varying degrees of resources (e.g., personnel and tools), role definition, and experience.

Revising the term "problems of practice" to gathering *practice-based evidence* (Green 2008) capitalizes on the shared expertise of school leaders and their corresponding insights by acknowledging diverse school circumstances. School leaders need shared expertise on *how* to implement the numerous new topics expected of them. A major goal of the networked leadership community is for individual principals to determine how to implement research-based practices. The collective wisdom of how to implement is the basis for creating practice-based evidence of what works in different school circumstances.

An example of a collegial network designed to assist medical professionals with the affective dimension of medicine is the previously noted Schwartz

Center Rounds program. The program offers health-care providers a regularly scheduled time to process the difficulties faced in modern medicine. Many physicians share two job characteristics faced by school principals:

1. isolation from encountering problems on their own, and
2. significant levels of professional burnout.

Recent studies (Chen 2011) of the medical professionals who attend Schwartz Rounds have shown attendees feel less stressed, are better able to cope, and discover new strategies for addressing difficult situations. The Schwartz Rounds process establishes a networked community of health-care providers that has purpose, processes for interacting, and goals.

Similarly, a networked leadership community for school leaders must provide answers to how the community is defined, why is it established, and how its members will interact. An effective networked leadership community explicitly identifies the purpose, goal, format, qualities, and processes that will be used. Table 7.4 notes these essential characteristics of an effective networked community for school leaders.

**Table 7.4.   Networked leadership community essential characteristics**

| | |
|---|---|
| Purpose | Expertise and insights are needed by a networked community because of diverse school circumstances, varying degrees of resources, personnel, tools, materials, role definitions, and experiences. |
| Goal | Determine how to implement research-based practices to improve student learning translated through practice-based evidence. |
| Format | Self-selected high-performing collaborative teams (trios or quads) meet face-to-face and through web-based interactions. |
| Qualities | The community must be trust based, supportive, and provide encouragement to influence self-efficacy. |
| Processes | It must include dialogue, discussion, working agreements, protocols for balanced interaction, P-P-P (pause, paraphrase, pose), goal setting, and feedback for learning and growth. |

As noted in table 7.4, the purpose of a networked leadership community is to share expertise and insights for implementation topics because principals are in diverse school circumstances. A collegial network established for principals recognizes that changes are often difficult and efficacious leaders need support in order to persist in the face of challenges.

## Effective Networked Leadership Communities

In effective networked leadership communities, principals self-select into high-performing teams of three or four with similar school characteristics or implementation topics. The principals self-select high-performing team members because of the communities' qualities of being trust based and supportive, and providing encouragement and feedback to influence self-efficacy. Self-selection by principals, informed by goals and established criteria, is important because trust and commitment are essential for full participation in a high-performing team.

The high-performing teams meet regularly face-to-face or virtually with other teams in the network, or with their team members. The processes used by high-performing teams in a networked leadership community are those described throughout this book. For example, some important processes used by high-performing teams include listening skills (e.g., pause-paraphrase-pose), techniques to enhance dialogue and discussion, goal setting, and feedback for growth and learning.

Developing this type of collegial network for support and feedback has numerous benefits. Having access to robust social networks actually has "protective effects" for maintaining both physical and psychological health. Professional isolation tends to be the norm for many school leaders, and collegial networks can reduce the effects of stress.

The busyness of the principalship, resulting in being overwhelmed, might appear to provide a convincing argument that there is little time available to participate in a networked leadership community. However, the potential positive impact of these networks on self-efficacy, often in short supply for principals—especially those with only a few years of experience—warrants the time required to develop and sustain engagement in these networks.

Networked leadership communities can sustain and contribute to longevity and increased job satisfaction. Albert Bandura (1994) asserts the power of social models that enhance self-efficacy. He states,

> Seeing people similar to oneself succeed by sustained effort raises observers' beliefs that they too possess the capabilities to master comparable activities required to succeed. People seek proficient models who possess the competencies to which they aspire. People who are persuaded verbally that they possess the capabilities to master given activities are likely to mobilize greater effort and sustain it than if they harbor self-doubts and dwell on personal deficiencies when problems arise. (71–72)

*Choreographed 1st time*
*2nd not cancelled*
*MS principals visited each others schools*

**SEEKING SUPPORT AND FEEDBACK FOR LEARNING    123**

## Relationship between Support and Resiliency and between Feedback and Excellence

A strong and supportive professional network actually contributes to a member's psychological well-being and can lead to resiliency. Figure 7.1 illustrates the important connection between support and resiliency and between feedback and excellence.

*Collegial network*
*mutual trust*

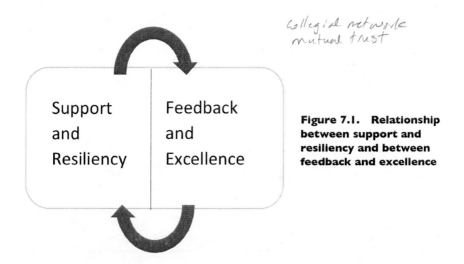

Support and Resiliency | Feedback and Excellence

**Figure 7.1.   Relationship between support and resiliency and between feedback and excellence**

Members of a professional network are capable of sharing expertise through carefully designed informative feedback so colleagues develop and refine effective leadership practices. Excellence is unattainable in the absence of feedback, and resiliency is unlikely without a network for encouragement and support. The collegial network is designed intentionally to assist principals with challenges, set professional goals for accomplishing difficult tasks, and provide feedback that offers expertise and insights for success.

School leaders need to learn to give and receive feedback utilizing the attributes of feedback for adult learning and growth. The informative feedback conversation focuses on developing a goal statement with action plans and steps. This is a two-way exchange of information. One approach that can be used is a future-oriented planning conversation that features clarifying steps and insights based on expertise from colleagues.

The disposition of seeking support and feedback for learning is critical for school leaders who frequently work in environments void of useful information that is communicated in a manner that helps to improve performance. Mutual trust is the foundation of any colleague-to-colleague relationship, especially when feedback is the focus.

## Professional Goal Setting

Effective networked leadership communities also engage leaders in the practice of setting and refining leadership goals related to implementation. Edwin Locke and Gary Latham (2002) have summarized thirty-five years of empirical research about goal setting. Goal setting works because it directs our attention to activities that will have an influence on the goal. The language that defines a goal needs to be specific and tangible because refrains such as "get better" or "improve your performance" are too vague, broad, and ambiguous. Ambitious goals lead to greater effort than goals that are set low.

Goal setting is a fundamental practice that is essential for the success of school leaders. Goal setting leads to intentional planning, and with support, guidance, and feedback from a networked leadership community, specific impactful strategies are adopted. Goals that are challenging and attainable draw upon efficacious behaviors such as persistence and flexibility. Goals that are selected and developed by school leaders, rather than assigned or delegated from above, lead to a greater level of commitment and motivation. School leaders are confronted with setting goals and questions such as follows:

- How clearly can you articulate school improvement goals to others both orally and in writing?
- By what target date should those goals be achieved?
- How will you make a commitment to working toward your goal over an extended period of time with a plan of action to reach your goal?
- What skills and knowledge are required to reach your goal?
- What do you need to know?
- What is your vision of what you are trying to achieve for yourself—your personal goal? Who will you be in your future?

Professional goal setting for principals in a collegial network has two components: (1) an implementation goal or *the what* is to be accomplished, and (2) a first-person leadership goal or *the how* that is based upon the capabilities and practices from the dispositions of leadership. To allow for specific feedback from colleagues in the networked leadership community, an implementation goal should be

- supported by research;
- clearly thought through;
- focused on improving the student learning environment; and
- described in a logic model format allowing for specific feedback from colleagues.

The accompanying goal statement should contain reasonable action plans, action steps, and realistic timelines. As an example, table 7.5 contains a goal statement with action plans and action steps that will allow colleagues to provide specific feedback based upon experience and expertise.

*School goals vs prof/personal goals*

**Table 7.5. Sample goal statement with action plans and action steps**

| Goal | Increase the graduation rate by goal setting with students while monitoring students at risk of dropping out of high school. |
|---|---|
| Action plan | Action steps |
| Implement a 4-year career planning cycle that meets the individual needs of students. | Administer interest inventory to all students. Statement of career goals, purpose, and interests developed by all students Current year action plan aligned to goal statement for each student completed during advisory class with quarterly check-ins |
| Implement drop-out early warning system to facilitate intervention for students at risk of dropping out. | Systematically and routinely use a comprehensive data system and easy-to-use reporting structures to identify students at risk of dropping out of high school. Each year, 75% of targeted teachers and staff members will have participated in professional development/training for using the early warning system. Or each year, 75% of targeted teachers and staff members will self-report that they are aware of and understand how to appropriately use the early warning system. Or by March 15th, 75% of targeted teachers and staff members will report having used the early warning system a minimum of three times to identify at-risk students and provide identified students with appropriate interventions. The numbers of students identified at risk of dropping out who receive academic and behavioral interventions will increase each year. |

The goal statement of increasing graduation rates will be an outcome of developing and monitoring student interest and progress through an action plan, as well as monitoring progress and crafting interventions for individual students. The goal statement in table 7.5 is supported by research.

John Hattie (2015) determined that response to intervention has a significant effect size. Russell Quaglia and Michael Corso (2014) determined that understanding students' interests is integral to a commitment to learning.

*Missin this* (handwritten note in margin)

A first-person leadership goal must focus on the specific steps that a school principal will take to accomplish the implementation goal. Many goal-setting processes led by principals focus on what *others* are going to do to accomplish goals. A first-person leadership goal focuses on what the principal will do to support an implementation goal.

In addition, a first-person leadership goal addresses *how* a school leader will influence, encourage, and support others to accomplish goals. (Note that the cycle-of-work calendar for a building leadership team as described in table 6.5 provides a template for designing a first-person leadership goal.) Feedback is a vital component of the goal-setting process. Feedback needs to be based upon expertise that is helpful and delivered with interpersonal communication practices that are known to be effective.

## CAPABILITY FOUR: CREATING FEEDBACK SPIRALS FOR CONTINUOUS INDIVIDUAL AND ORGANIZATIONAL SELF-LEARNING

Once a goal is established in a collegial setting and implemented in collaboration with the staff at a school, feedback must be sought. A feedback spiral, as noted in figure 7.2, is an important model for goal setting. Feed-

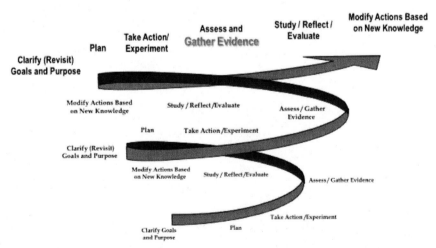

**Figure 7.2.   A sample feedback spiral.** *Costa and Kallick* **(1995, 27).**

back, collecting information, and revising action steps becomes a routine and predictable way of setting and adjusting goals. These spirals depend on a variety of sources of information.

Those directly involved in change at the school collect specific kinds of evidence about what is happening in the organization's environment. Once these data are analyzed, interpreted, and internalized, individuals modify their actions to more closely achieve the organization's goals. Thus, individuals—and the organization—are continually self-learning, self-renewing, and self-modifying. Each element along the feedback spiral in figure 7.2 is described below:

- *Clarify goals and purposes.* What is the purpose for what you are doing? What beliefs or values does it reflect? What outcomes would you expect as a result of your actions?
- *Plan.* What actions would you take to achieve the desired outcomes? How would you set up an experiment to test your ideas? What evidence would you collect to help inform you about the results of your actions? What would you look for as indicators your outcomes were or were not achieved? How will you leave the door open for other discoveries and possibilities that were not built into the original design? What process will you put in place that will help you describe what actually happened?
- *Take action/experiment.* Execute the plan.
- *Assess/gather evidence.* Implement assessment strategies during (ongoing and formative) and at some point after (summative), upon conclusion or some stopping point.
- *Study, reflect, evaluate.* Whether this is an individual or organizational change, how are the results congruent with stated values, intentions, and goals? What meaning can be made of the data? Who might serve as a critical colleague to facilitate or mediate your learning from this experience? What have individuals learned from this action?
- *Modify actions based on new knowledge.* What will be done differently in the future as a result of reflection and integration of new knowledge? Is this plan worth trying again?
- *Revisit and clarify goals and purposes.* Do the goals still make sense? Are they still of value, or do they need to be redefined, refocused, or refined? This element returns to the first step in the spiral: clarify goals and purposes.

To develop the habit of remaining open to continuous learning, the school community gathers data through conscious observation of feelings, attitudes, and skills; through observation and interviews with others; and by collecting evidence showing the effects of their efforts on the environment. These data are analyzed, interpreted, and internalized. Based on this analysis, the organization, or individuals, modifies actions to more closely achieve the goals. Thus, individuals and the organization become continually self-learning, self-renewing, and self-modifying (Costa and Kallick 2004).

Setting an implementation goal with action plans and steps and a leadership goal in a collegial setting is critical to the ongoing success of school leaders. A supportive collegial environment can offer expertise through modeling and feedback. The feedback spiral is useful as a framework for seeking feedback from members of a school community.

## Receiving Feedback

Receiving feedback is not always easy. It is sometimes hard to hear and to accept, as it may touch a nerve. It takes openness, a strong sense of efficacy, and a growth mindset in order to receive and learn from feedback. A useful strategy when receiving feedback and before taking any action is to pause, take time, and contemplate the meaning in the message, in an effort to improve oneself (Porter 2016).

## Giving Feedback

Creating an effective feedback spiral for continuous individual and organizational self-learning also requires school leaders to give feedback. Effective school leaders not only seek feedback but also know how to deliver feedback with skill and impact. When leaders model giving constructive feedback as a process, others will soon learn and follow. First and foremost, a relationship of trust must exist (see chapter 3). Some criteria for giving effective feedback (Costa and Garmston 2015) include the following:

- Feedback must be neutral. If it carries value judgments, such as "good" or "poor," it tends to stop thinking. It increases the dependence on external feedback and diminishes the capacity for accurate self-reflection.
- Receptivity for feedback is improved if it is quantitative, based on previously agreed indicators of standards of excellence.
- Evaluative feedback makes the least contribution to learning and behavior change.

- People need feedback so desperately that, in the absence of actual feedback, they will often invent it.
- Data energize learning. Humans learn and grow when they have the opportunity to consider external and internal data.
- External data are useful for learning if feedback is frequent, timely, and stated in constructive terms. Feedback given too long after an assessment or learning event will not influence a learner in the same way as data offered almost immediately.
- Learners need opportunities to generate data and to self-evaluate in order to become self-directed. They must learn how to compare their current performance to previous performances, and they must learn how to analyze their performance in terms of personal goals for effective performance.

Skilled and purposeful feedback is the foundation of growth and purposeful change. Giving feedback in a clear and actionable style is the responsibility and obligation of leaders. Employing the criteria above in both classrooms and organizations is a great way for leaders to foster a commitment to feedback.


## SUMMARY

Three important capabilities of seeking support and feedback for learning are (1) developing self-knowledge, self-awareness, and self-efficacy while maintaining a sense of humility; (2) frequently seeking feedback focused on learning and growth; and (3) engaging in a networked leadership community of high-performing teams of principals.

Principals are well served by having an understanding of the intrapersonal dimension because it is integral to learning as a leader. Engaging in a network of colleagues for encouragement and support has a protective effect against the isolation and burnout many principals identify as reasons for leaving the profession.


## MIDDLE SCHOOL VIGNETTE

Three principals had formed a high-performing team during a statewide networked leadership community professional-learning institute. Oscar, Raquel, and Kimberly decided to work together for three specific reasons:

1. Each of the three led the only middle school in their district.
2. They wanted to reduce professional isolation and seek feedback from trusted colleagues.
3. And they wanted to learn to apply information about providing feedback to adults.

All three principals were at different stages of implementing the new mandated teacher evaluation system. The emphasis in the training had been on data collection and assigning a score to each teacher on the different evaluation rubrics. Oscar, Raquel, and Kimberly were over the initial phase of feeling overwhelmed by having to spend significantly more time observing teachers in classrooms. They had shared insights into how to streamline both the data-collection process and data entry into a web-based scoring system. They felt it was time to focus on improving their skills at providing feedback that teachers found was useful.

Raquel suggested they use the "Attributes of Feedback for Adult Learning and Growth" guidelines (table 7.3) as a starting point for their conversations. She was keenly aware of the pitfalls of providing feedback that felt judgmental and personal. Raquel shared one of her fundamental motivations for becoming a principal was bad experiences she had had previously as a teacher being evaluated by a poorly trained principal.

Kimberly confided that she had asked her staff for feedback the previous school year. One major theme mentioned by teachers was having conversations that were more collaborative and two-way in nature. Oscar shared he really liked the idea of modeling *feedback for adult learning and growth* since many of his teachers seemed receptive to working together in teams.

Oscar, Raquel, and Kimberly decided to focus on providing feedback that is specific, manageable, factual, and alterable. All three agreed to ask selected teachers about how they delivered feedback during evaluation conversations. Furthermore, they decided to develop or locate a set of *effective questions or language stems* that could be used to promote collaborative conversations with teachers.

## QUESTIONS TO ENGAGE YOUR THINKING AND DISCUSSION WITH COLLEAGUES

1. What are some opportunities for you to receive feedback about your role as a leader? What topic might you ask a colleague about for feedback?

2. Which statements in table 7.3 (attributes of feedback for adult learning and growth) resonate with you? Why?
3. How might you incorporate one of the attributes into your next conversation with a teacher or colleague?

## REFERENCES

Bandura, A. (1994). Self-efficacy. In V. S. Ramachaudran (Ed.), *Encyclopedia of human behavior* (Vol. 4, pp. 71–81). New York: Academic Press. (Reprinted in H. Friedman [Ed.], *Encyclopedia of mental health*. San Diego: Academic Press, 1998).

Chen, P. (2011, September 15). Sharing the stresses of being a doctor. *New York Times*, D6.

Costa, A. (2001). *Developing minds: A resource book for teaching thinking*. Alexandria, VA: Association for Supervision and Curriculum Development.

Costa, A., and Garmston, R. (2015). *Cognitive coaching: Developing self-directed leaders and learners* (3rd Ed.). Lanham, MD: Rowman & Littlefield.

Costa, A., and Kallick, B. (1995). *Assessment in the learning organization: Shifting the paradigm*. Alexandria, VA: Association for Supervision and Curriculum Development.

———. (2004). *Assessment Strategies for Self-Directed Learning*. Thousand Oaks, CA: Corwin Press.

Donaldson, G. (2008). *How leaders learn: Cultivating capacitates for school improvement*. New York: Teachers College Press.

Green, L. (2008). Making research relevant: If it is an evidence-based practice, where's the practice-based evidence? In *Family Practice, 25* (suppl. 1), i20–i24.

Hattie, J. (2009). *Visible learning: A synthesis of over 800 meta-analyses relating to achievement*. New York: Routledge.

———. (2015). Hattie ranking: 195 influences and effect sizes related to student achievement. Visible Learning. Retrieved from http://visible-learning.org/.

Kluger, A. N., and DeNisi, A. S. (1996). The effects of feedback interventions on performance: A historical review, a meta-analysis, and a preliminary feedback intervention theory. *Psychological Bulletin, 119*(2), 254–284.

Locke, E. A., and Latham, G. P. (2002). Building a practically useful theory of goal setting and task motivation: A 35-year odyssey. *American Psychologist, 57*(9), 705–717. Retrieved from https://www.researchgate.net/.

Markow, D., Macia, L., and Lee, B. (2012). *The MetLife Survey of the American Teacher: Challenges for School Leadership*. New York: MetLife.

Ozbay, F., Johnson, D., Dimoulas, E., Morgan, C. A., Charney, D., and Southwick, S. (2007). Social support and resilience to stress: From neurobiology to clinical practice. *Psychiatry (Edgmont), 4*(5), 35–40.

Porter, J. G. (2016, March 24). Feedback: Lean in or back away? Pulse, March 19, 2016. Retrieved from https://www.linkedin.com/.

Prime, J., and Salib, E. (2014). Inclusive leadership: The view from six countries. New York: Catalyst Research.

Quaglia, R., and Corso, M. (2014). *Student voice: The instrument of change*. Thousand Oaks, CA: Corwin.

Robinson, V. (2011). *Student-centered leadership*. San Francisco: Jossey-Bass.

School Leaders Network. (2014). CHURN: The high cost of principal turnover. Retrieved from https://connectleadsucceed.org/.

Scullen, S. E., Mount, M. K., and Goff, M. (2000). Understanding the latent structure of job performance ratings. *Journal of Applied Psychology, 85*(6), 956–970.

Tyre, P. (2015, September 26). Why do more than half of principals quit after five years? Hechinger Report. Retrieved from http://hechingerreport.org/.

Waldinger, R. (2015). What makes a good life? Lessons from the longest study on happiness. Retrieved from TED. https://www.ted.com/.

Wiliam, D. (2011). *Embedded formative assessment*. Bloomington, IN: Solution Tree Press.

## 8

# PURSUING ADAPTIVE COMPETENCE

The human body is river of intelligence, energy and information that is constantly renewing itself in every second of its existence.

—Deepak Chopra

In architecture, a keystone is the wedge-shaped stone placed at the apex of a masonry arch. It is the final piece placed during construction and locks all the stones into position. An arch cannot be self-supporting until the keystone is placed. Figuratively, the term refers to a central element—an idea, policy, or concept upon which other associated elements rely in order to function. It locks other components in place so the entire structure is stable and functions as designed. It allows the whole to be self-supporting.

This chapter will focus on *pursuing adaptive competence* as the keystone disposition for the five dispositions of leadership. Pursuing adaptive competence is defined as incorporating into practice the metacognitive processes, intrapersonal skills, and cognitive flexibility needed to effectively diagnose, plan for, reflect on, and learn from solving complex problems. A leader must be able to plan, problem solve, reflect, and diagnose while flexibly transferring knowledge and skills acquired from previous experiences. Leaders in the information age will encounter problems where solutions are not readily apparent, including situations where even framing the appropriate questions that describe the situation can be ambiguous.

Like a keystone, the disposition of pursuing adaptive competence locks the other four dispositions into place and allows the overall model of educational leadership presented in this book to be self-supporting. This chapter provides an overview of adaptive competence, followed by a discussion of the three capabilities of pursuing adaptive competence:

1. using self-managing, self-monitoring, and self-modifying skills to inform behaviors and actions;
2. engaging flexibly in thinking and behaviors; and
3. solving complex problems and addressing adaptive challenges.

Pursuing adaptive competence, the keystone disposition for leadership in schools, requires the *activation* of the four previously discussed dispositions simultaneously with these three capabilities. The chapter will also provide a middle school vignette that illustrates the disposition and associated capabilities of pursuing adaptive competence and suggest questions to engage the reader's thinking and discussion with colleagues.

## WHAT IS ADAPTIVE COMPETENCE?

Many cognitive scientists who investigate the nature of learning agree that adaptive competence is an ultimate goal of learning. The low-road/high-road theory (Perkins and Salomon 1988) is a useful place to begin a discussion about adaptive competence because it pertains to the transfer of learning.

- *Low-road transfer* refers to developing basic knowledge or skills that can be transferred through repetition and practice.
- *High-road transfer* refers to an analysis of a situation and determining which strategies learned previously might apply to the new setting.

Examples of low-road transfer might be a child learning to tie shoes or an adolescent learning to brake and steer an automobile. For school leaders, examples of low-road transfer might include learning the state and district processes and procedures for adopting a new curriculum, or aligning a new curriculum with state standards. These types of rote learning are not the focus of adaptive competence.

In contrast, adaptive competence focuses on high-road transfer. High-road transfer depends on making choices while drawing upon experience. In the case of the adolescent noted above who is learning to drive, an example of high-road transfer might be driving in hazardous, icy weather. In this situation, the adolescent needs to continuously analyze road conditions and determine the best strategy for safe driving for each condition.

An example of adaptive competence related to school leaders might be members of a school-district leadership team proposing numerous options for incorporating a dual language program and instructional strategies into an existing English/language arts curriculum for grades prekindergarten through 12. In this situation, the leadership team needs to engage in an iterative process of assessing current strengths and gaps within the existing English/language arts curriculum, identifying the learning needs of students, and developing strategies for effectively integrating the dual language program in a manner that meets district priorities and positively impacts student learning.

Adaptive competence is further refined by exploring the distinction between veridical decision making and adaptive decision making. Elkhonon Goldberg and Kenneth Podell (1999) made the distinction between veridical decision making and adaptive decision making for their colleagues in cognitive psychology and neuropsychology. Many, if not most, decisions made by school leaders will require this latter type of adaptive decision making as opposed to veridical decision making.

- *Veridical decision making* is about providing the correct response; the answer is independent of and external to the person responding because it is fact based. Veridical is taken from *veritas*, the Latin word for truth.
- *Adaptive decision making* is dependent on the priorities set by the person responding. Adaptive decision making relies on choices informed through previous learning.

Therefore, in summary, adaptive competence can be understood as learning that requires a high-road transfer of knowledge and skills to new settings and contexts. In addition, adaptive competence requires adaptive decision making that relies on choices informed by this previous learning.

## PURSUING ADAPTIVE COMPETENCE IN AMBIGUOUS ENVIRONMENTS

Goldberg (2009) observes that "most 'executive leadership' decisions are priority based, made in ambiguous environments, and adaptive, rather than veridical, in nature" (100). Making decisions in complex environments fraught with ambiguity requires selecting priorities, discerning the questions that need answers, and identifying potential solutions.

Pursuing adaptive competence includes strategically drawing upon one, some, or all five dispositions of leadership that are needed at the time to best address the situation. As dilemmas present themselves, leaders step to the balcony and carefully consider the situation. As Ronald Heifetz and Donald Laurie (1997) point out, the balcony view is especially important when "adaptive challenges" may be present within the dilemma at hand.

Without the capacity to move back and forth between the field of action and the balcony, to reflect day to day, moment to moment, on the many ways in which an organization's habits can sabotage adaptive work, a leader easily and unwittingly becomes a prisoner of the system. The dynamics of adaptive changes are far too complex to keep track of, let alone influence, if leaders stay only on the field of play (Heifetz and Laurie 1997, 125–126).

An important aspect of activating adaptive competence in complex environments is the ability to examine dilemmas and ambiguous situations through a diagnostic lens. *Diagnosis*, the ability to assess a situation from the balcony, begins with exploring the questions that need to be answered. An essential component of diagnosing, and a step that is often overlooked, is clearly formulating the questions that one is attempting to answer. Table 8.1 provides examples of the types of questions that can be asked as part of the diagnostic process in ambiguous, unstructured, or complex environments often encountered by school leaders.

**Table 8.1.  Diagnosis and attributes of adaptability in complex environments**

| Nature of situation | Attributes of adaptability | Diagnosis (What is the question or situation?) |
|---|---|---|
| Ambiguous | Flexible | What are possible alternatives? |
| Unstructured | Self-modifying | Which alternatives can be applied? |
| Complex | Apply previous knowledge in new or novel setting | Which alternatives should be applied? |

Leaders may need to delay making final decisions while first clarifying the questions that need to be addressed, gathering adequate information, and exploring potential solutions. There is often a tendency in leadership to apply solutions that have worked in the past and not consider the current context and values of the new situation (Heifetz, Grashow, and Linsky 2009). Delaying action and exercising a diagnostic lens requires self-discipline and the ability to draw upon intrapersonal skills. Delaying action and exercising a diagnostic lens tempers the impulse to act with the patience needed to effectively address complex problems.

## CAPABILITY ONE: USING SELF-MANAGING, SELF-MONITORING, AND SELF-MODIFYING SKILLS TO INFORM BEHAVIORS AND ACTIONS

The self-schema is a multifaceted phenomenon that refers to the beliefs or ideas about one's self that influence behavior. The concept of self-schema was introduced in the previous chapter as it related to the intrapersonal dimension of leadership. This chapter calls upon a different self-schema as it pertains to adaptive competence.

Adaptive competence requires one to assess and act upon current circumstances and also requires the ability to make adjustments based on situational cues. More specifically, pursuing adaptive competence requires individuals to draw upon the schema of self-managing, self-monitoring, and self-modifying to respond effectively in environments or situations that are ambiguous, unstructured, or complex. Each of these three self-schema is described below:

- *Self-managing*: knowing the significance of (and being inclined to) approach tasks with outcomes clearly in mind, a strategic plan, and necessary data, in addition to drawing from past experiences, anticipating success indicators, and creating alternatives for accomplishment.
- *Self-monitoring*: having sufficient self-knowledge about what works; establishing conscious metacognitive strategies for in-the-moment indicators of whether the strategic plan is working or not; and assisting in the decision-making processes of altering the plan and choosing the right actions and strategies.
- *Self-modifying*: reflecting on, evaluating, analyzing, and constructing meaning from experiences and making a commitment to apply the learning to future activities, tasks, and challenges (Costa and Garmston 2015).

As leaders pursue adaptive competence, they have a sense of deliberativeness because they think before they act. These leaders are *self-managing*, intentionally forming a vision of a product, plan of action, goal, or destination before taking action. Self-managing leaders strive to clarify and understand directions, develop a strategy for approaching a problem, and withhold immediate value judgments before fully understanding an idea.

Leaders pursue adaptive competence by *self-monitoring* and considering alternatives and consequences of several possible directions prior to taking action. These self-monitoring leaders listen to alternative points of view and decrease the need for trial and error by consciously gathering information and taking time to reflect on an answer before giving it. These leaders are aware of their own behaviors and the effects of their actions on others and the environment.

Effective leaders pursuing adaptive competence are also *self-modifying*, consciously monitoring the effectiveness of their problem-solving strategies and employing alternatives if these strategies are ineffective. They regularly assess the clarity of their goals and the effectiveness of the strategies they employ to resolve problems and achieve goals.

Self-modifying also requires leaders to gather feedback to accurately consider the need to self-modify behaviors and actions. Formative feedback (formally or informally) provides information to leaders regarding effectiveness with communication, goal setting, vision, biases, and congruence between actions and beliefs. Once feedback is gathered and considered, leaders who are adaptively competent regularly modify behaviors and actions as needed based on this formative feedback.

The trilogy of self-managing, self-monitoring, and self-modifying skills also requires leaders to be effective questioners. As part of the problem-solving process, effective questioners know how to ask questions to fill in the gaps between what they know and what they do not know. Effective questioners are inclined to ask a range of questions that potentially explore the breadth and depth of an issue. Some examples of this type of questioning in adaptive situations might include those noted in table 8.2.

**Table 8.2.   Questions asked in an adaptive situation**

| | |
|---|---|
| Data questions | How might we confirm this evidence either quantitatively or qualitatively? |
| | To what degree do we understand the information from this data source? |
| Multiple perspectives | From which viewpoint are we seeing, reading, or hearing? |
| | From what angle, what perspective, might we consider this situation? |
| Problem solving | What do you think would happen *if . . . ?"* |
| | *If* true, then what might happen when . . . ?" |

When confronted with a new and perplexing problem, leaders pursuing adaptive competence draw from their past experiences and gather further information in order to more deeply understand the challenge before them.

They can often be heard to say, "This reminds me of . . ." or, "This dilemma has some similar attributes to the one we faced . . ."

These leaders pursuing adaptive competence explain what they are doing now in terms of analogies with or references to previous experiences. They call upon their store of knowledge and experience as a part of the multiple data sources to support theories to explain or processes to solve each new challenge. Furthermore, they are able to abstract meaning from one experience, carry it forth, and apply it in a new and novel situations.

## CAPABILITY TWO: ENGAGING FLEXIBLY IN THINKING AND BEHAVIORS

Leaders who think flexibly are able to shift, at will, through multiple perceptual positions. Flexible leaders can approach a problem from a new angle using a novel approach. Edward de Bono (1970, 300) refers to this as *lateral thinking*. Thus, flexibility of mind is essential for working with social diversity, enabling an individual to recognize the wholeness and distinctness of other people's ways of experiencing and making meaning.

The capability of engaging flexibly in thinking and behaviors includes the ability to adjust one's thinking and seek novel approaches. First, engaging flexibly requires leaders to *adjust thinking* based on additional data or reasoning, even if (or perhaps especially if) the data and reasoning contradict the leader's own beliefs or thinking. Leaders who are engaging flexibly need to consider alternative points of view and be able to effectively deal with several sources of information simultaneously. Therefore, effective leaders will intentionally seek out and listen to points of view, opinions, and approaches that may be different than their own.

Second, engaging flexibly requires leaders to acquire a *full repertoire of flexibility with perceptual views*. These leaders flexibly deploy problem-solving strategies and, as needed, broaden perspectives when employing detailed precision thinking. For example, leaders who are engaging flexibly will intentionally seek out the points of view and perspectives of less vocal and visible staff members.

In addition, the full repertoire of flexibility with perceptual views includes being able to flexibly move between a balcony view and dance-floor view in problem solving and decision making. Effective leaders use the balcony view as needed to discern themes and patterns from numerous sources of information, while also employing the dance-floor view as needed to examine the individual and sometimes minute parts that make up the whole.

Finally, the capability of engaging flexibly in thinking and behaviors requires leaders to *seek novel approaches*. To engage flexibly, leaders need to be open to changing their approaches, behaviors, or ways of thinking. Solving problems in the information age means that often the area of the challenge is not well defined, with unclear pathways and methods for solution.

In these types of situations with unclear pathways, effective leaders use a creative approach that engages imagination, as well as intelligence. Seeking novel approaches requires leaders to reflect on alternative ways of responding before reacting to a situation, and to avoid habitual responses. Leaders who engage flexibly seek many, varied, and even unusual ideas that have high potential to address a problem in a novel and valuable way.

## CAPABILITY THREE: SOLVING COMPLEX PROBLEMS AND ADDRESSING ADAPTIVE CHALLENGES

One of the characteristics that distinguish humans from other forms of life is our inclination and ability to *find* problems to solve. By definition, a problem is any stimulus, task, phenomenon, or discrepancy, the explanation for which is not immediately known. When leaders experience dichotomies, are confused by dilemmas, or come face-to-face with uncertainties, their most effective actions require drawing forth certain patterns of intellectual behavior to resolve the discrepancies.

What is unique about leaders pursuing adaptive competence is their capacity to draw forth certain intellectual dispositions under challenging conditions. When these adaptively competent leaders encounter problems, they are intrigued by and lend themselves to resolving challenging situations. Adaptively competent leaders display capacities for strategic reasoning, insightfulness, perseverance, creativity, and craftsmanship. Through reflection, adaptively competent leaders construct meaning from experiences and accumulate strategies, maps, and procedures that are then applied in future problem-solving situations.

Pursuing adaptive competence is particularly important in the information age given that educators will regularly face complex problems. Leaders focused on developing the disposition of pursuing adaptive competence will

- confront problems with confidence,
- deploy strategic approaches,
- set realistic and clear goals, and
- design strategies to achieve goals.

A major goal of effective leaders should be to make their school and classrooms *problem friendly* and to welcome problems. Leaders who are adaptively competent overcome the impulse to immediately come up with a solution. Acting upon one's initial impulse places the solution at the beginning of the process, when the solution should come after deliberation and data gathering—toward the end of the process. Furthermore, it might be determined that what was thought to be the problem was not a real problem.

The steps in problem solving are never static or sequential. Leaders pursuing adaptive competence delay forming an immediate solution because they rely on a *mental map* of gathering information, generating possible solutions, and developing a plan. Table 8.3 illustrates a mental map for solving complex problems.

**Table 8.3. Mental map for solving complex problems**

| | |
|---|---|
| Gathering information | Build background knowledge about the problem by identifying and becoming clearer about the issues, reading what experts say. |
| | Gather opinions and feedback from multiple, diverse sources before making significant decisions. |
| | Understand technical problems/adaptive challenges. |
| | Unbundle aspects of the problem while keeping the whole in mind. |
| Generating possible solutions | Take what you know and apply it in a novel setting (establish an environment for generating numerous questions from multiple perspectives). |
| | Use brainstorming and other generative strategies. |
| | Think flexibly regarding potential ideas and suggestions. Evaluate and predict the consequences of each of those possible solutions. |
| Developing a plan | Decide on strategies for monitoring and evaluating solutions. |
| | Document the agreements; invite commitments. |
| | Generate and agree on contingencies as conditions change. |

The information age requires the heightened ability to think and problem solve in concert with others, and to be increasingly more interdependent and sensitive to the needs of others. Problem solving has become so complex that no one person can go it alone. No one has access to all the data needed to make critical decisions; no one person can consider as many alternatives as several people can. It takes the combined ingenuity, perceptions, strategies, experiences, and interactions of groups of thinkers to solve problems today. Cooperative humans realize that all of us together are more powerful, intellectually and physically, than any one individual.

Working in groups also requires the ability to justify ideas and to test the feasibility of solution strategies with others. It requires the development of a willingness and openness to accept feedback from others. Through this interaction, the group and the individual continue to grow. Listening, consensus seeking, giving up an idea to work with someone else's, empathy, compassion, group leadership, knowing how to support group efforts, and altruism all are practices indicative of cooperative human beings.

## SUMMARY

Adaptive competence is the keystone disposition because a school leader must be able to plan, problem solve, reflect, and diagnose in the present while transferring knowledge and skills acquired from previous experiences. This chapter explored the keystone disposition of pursuing adaptive competence and discussed each of the three associated capabilities: (1) using self-managing, self-monitoring, and self-modifying skills to inform behaviors; (2) engaging flexibly in thinking and behaviors; and (3) solving complex problems and addressing adaptive challenges.

Contemporary leaders in the information age are regularly placed in situations that require adaptive competence. Because the environment in which educational leaders work is often ambiguous and nonroutine, leaders must diagnose the current situation and generate solutions for improving student learning.

## MIDDLE SCHOOL VIGNETTE

In chapter 7, three principals had formed a high-performing team during a statewide networked leadership community professional-learning institute. Oscar, Raquel, and Kimberly decided to work together for three specific reasons:

1. All three led the only middle school in their district.
2. They wanted to reduce professional isolation and seek feedback from trusted colleagues.
3. And they wanted to learn to apply information about providing feedback to adults.

They met online four weeks after agreeing to improve the use of feedback in their respective schools. A protocol was in place for online conversations, so each principal had ample time during the ninety-minute session to share progress or dilemmas.

Oscar was the first to share, and he reported that introducing feedback to teachers had not gone as well as he had hoped. He was an accomplished and experienced principal. The staff he had led previously was younger and less experienced and often enthusiastic about new ideas. Oscar discovered that seasoned and experienced staff members, though receptive to new ideas, were more reluctant, and a few teachers would openly and publicly challenge him. Oscar confided in Raquel and Kimberly that he was not really sure of his next steps. He shared that the processes and methods he used at his former middle school did not seem to be working.

Raquel and Kimberly took turns during the next fifteen minutes paraphrasing some of Oscar's comments and asking questions to clarify his strategy for using feedback with teachers. Based on the conversation with his two trusted colleagues, Oscar decided that the strategy he had used in his former middle school needed adjustment. It was not the first time the current staff had reacted with skepticism to one of his ideas.

Oscar now understood, having spent a little time examining the situation from the *balcony view*, that some elements that had worked in the *past* might be helpful if combined with an approach that would work in the *present*. Oscar discovered that being flexible and considering a different approach did not mean he was wishy-washy or indecisive. Kimberly shared that her staff members confided they felt *listened to* when she *massaged* a decision by regrouping and making adjustments.

Oscar's one big takeaway from his conversation with Raquel and Kimberly was he really needed a new *mental map* for solving problems. He did not have a *specific solution* from talking with Raquel and Kimberly. It was clear to him that he had many fine teachers he could rely on to assist in developing a plan for using feedback to improve adult and student learning.

## QUESTIONS TO ENGAGE YOUR THINKING AND DISCUSSION WITH COLLEAGUES

1. In what ways might you incorporate the data questions and multiple perspectives noted in table 8.2?
2. Many successful leaders report they use *cues* (such as push back a little from a table or decide to listen and not respond unless absolutely

necessary) to go to the balcony to gain a broader perspective. What cues might you adopt to leave the dance floor and get to the balcony?
3. How might the *mental map* noted in table 8.3 assist you when encountering a complex problem?

## REFERENCES

Costa, A., and Garmston, R. (2015). *Cognitive coaching: Developing self-directed leaders and learners* (3rd Ed.). Lanham, MD: Rowman & Littlefield.

de Bono, E. (1970). *Lateral thinking: Creativity step by step.* New York: Harper & Row.

Goldberg, E. (2009). *The new executive brain: Frontal lobes in a complex world.* New York: Oxford University Press.

Goldberg, E., and Podell, K. (1999). Adaptive versus veridical decision making and the frontal lobes. *Consciousness and Cognition, 8*(3), 364–377.

Heifetz, R. A., Grashow, A., and Linsky, M. (2009). *The practice of adaptive leadership: Tools and tactics for changing your organization and the world.* Boston: Harvard Business Press.

Heifetz, R. A., and Laurie, D. L. (1997). The work of leadership. *Harvard Business Review, 125,* 124–134.

Perkins, D., and Salomon, G. (1988). Teaching for transfer. *Educational Leadership, 46,* 22–32.

# DISCOVERING LEADERSHIP POTENTIAL IN AN AGILE ORGANIZATION

What you have to do and the way you have to do it is incredibly simple. Whether you are willing to do it, that's another matter.

—Peter Drucker

**T**he information age requires a different approach for leading in medicine, business, the military, and education. Leaders in all fields encounter challenges that defy solving problems by using predetermined steps that are transmitted to subordinates who comply with the directions as given. Bureaucratic command-and-control thinking, created for the industrial age, falls short of the agile thinking needed by leaders in the information age. The challenges are frequently nonroutine and can be solved only in a collaborative fashion, seeking information from multiple sources while empowering those closest to the problem to develop a solution.

Agile leaders apply a diagnostic lens to assess a situation accurately before deciding on a course of action or relying on a solution from a previous experience. Agility is achieved by nurturing the thinking, capabilities, and practices that can be deployed by thoughtful members of the organization. This chapter will conclude with a vignette that illustrates the application of capabilities drawn from the five dispositions of leadership.

Historically, leaders in education have labored in a valiant effort to follow and apply leadership suggestions from a variety of fields including business, cognitive science, and the military. As mentioned in previous chapters, school leaders now have access to an evidence base that points the way to leadership practices that are specific in nature for influencing improved student learning. Until recently, those specific skills, practices, and capabilities deployed by school-level leaders were not well researched or understood. The response to defining leadership in the information age in education must be twofold:

1. Revise or replace the leadership styles and practices used in education borrowed from other disciplines.
2. Focus on the leadership practices that influence student learning.

School leaders learn, grow, and develop in the cognitive (knowledge), interpersonal (relationships), and intrapersonal (self) dimensions (Donaldson 2008). These dimensions are incorporated and integrated into the five dispositions of leadership and form a coherent framework for the information age. The dispositions are further defined by the capabilities and practices that form a repertoire of options that can deployed given the circumstances.

The five dispositions of leadership were developed for leaders who have been searching for effective ways of addressing complex problems while improving the learning environment for all students. In this book, five dispositions of leadership have been identified and described the five dispositions of leadership. They are as follows:

1. *Thinking and acting interdependently*: promoting a positive, collaborative learning culture through distributed leadership.
2. *Communicating to influence*: developing the interpersonal skills to influence, mobilize, and motivate individuals and groups.
3. *Gathering and applying information for change*: utilizing data-based evidence to make decisions and provide formative feedback for setting direction and planning change.
4. *Seeking support and feedback for learning*: fostering personal/professional growth and resiliency.
5. *Pursuing adaptive competence* (keystone disposition): incorporating into practice metacognition and cognitive flexibility to effectively plan, reflect, diagnose, and solve complex problems.

These dispositions also serve as lenses and filters for observing, understanding, diagnosing, and strengthening organizational conditions and fostering learning of staff members as well as one's own self-discovery. As these dispositions become more apparent, positive effects may be observed in

(1) the culture of the agile organization, (2) the staff and students, and (3) yourself as a leader.

The five dispositions of leadership serve as references for mindful decision making. Confronted with unique, complex, problematic situations, these dispositions serve as an internal compass. Mindful school leaders use their executive processes to carefully, metacognitively employ one or more of these five dispositions by asking themselves, What is the most *thoughtful* action I can do right now? For example, questions for engaging each of the five dispositions of leadership include the following:

1. Thinking and acting interdependently
   - How does this problem affect others?
   - Where does the expertise lie within our school related to this dilemma?
   - How can we solve it together, and what can we learn from others that would help us to become better problem solvers?
   - What might educators potentially need to give up or let go of in order to think and act interdependently?
2. Influencing through effective communication
   - What communications might serve the situation well?
   - How might communication be developed to assist with creating trust and confidence in the problem-solving process?
   - How might I ensure congruence between communications and actions so there is confidence in the work ahead?
3. Gathering and applying information for change
   - How might I/we illuminate this problem to make it clearer, more precise?
   - Do I need to check out assumptions and data sources?
   - How might I break this problem down into its component parts and develop a strategy for understanding and accomplishing each step?
   - What further information may need to be gathered to assist us with potential solutions?
4. Seeking support and feedback for learning
   - What do I know or not know; what questions do I need to ask that would provide feedback regarding this dilemma?
   - What am I aware of in terms of my own beliefs, biases, values, and goals with this problem?
   - Who might be able to provide me with feedback on potential pitfalls, areas of success, and precise thinking on this issue?

5. Pursuing adaptive competence
   - How might I approach this problem flexibly?
   - How might I look at the situation in another way?
   - How can I draw upon my repertoire of problem-solving strategies?
   - How can I look at this problem from a fresh perspective and through the eyes of others who are affected by this situation?

The successful school district in the information age will need to set direction and provide the resources of time and focus. District leaders in an agile organization design opportunities for modeling, teaching, and utilizing the five dispositions of leadership. It is recognized that complex problems are addressed by highly competent leaders in small groups designed to do what bureaucratic organizations cannot: adapt and respond in productive ways to unique circumstances.

Creating a networked leadership community of principals arranged in high-performing teams to share insights and expertise is achieved within one school district or across a geographic region. The networked leadership community provides the opportunity to reduce isolation and create a powerful identity. Growth as a leader is *accelerated* when working with colleagues collaboratively.

Effectively exploring the aforementioned questions with trusted colleagues requires self-knowledge, self-awareness, inhibition of impulse, management of internal thought processes, being alert to situational cues, skillfully employing capacities, and gathering feedback about results. Learning and applying the dispositions of leadership take time, practice, feedback, reflection, a positive sense of self-efficacy, and encouragement from colleagues.

Agility within a school district is achieved when practice-based evidence is shared about implementation dilemmas in order to understand what successes and difficulties are being experienced in the field. School leaders meet in high-performing teams to share expertise and practice-based evidence while gaining insight into implementation difficulties and successes.

The five dispositions of leadership inform *how* a school leader applies the insights gained from practice-based evidence given their unique circumstances. Successful implementation of new and challenging topics requires positive self-efficacy as a leader, combined with the collective wisdom of practice-based evidence. Self-efficacy is increased when principals interact with colleagues who successfully implement topics similar to their own and are encouraged verbally to persist. Table 9.1 describes conditions that promote agility for school leaders.

**Table 9.1.  Conditions that promote agility**

| | |
|---|---|
| High-performing team | Colleagues committed to share, provide, and receive support and feedback, either face-to-face or virtually |
| Practice-based evidence | Insights and expertise collected and shared about an important research-based implementation topic |
| 5 dispositions of leadership | The many choices for *how to* implement practice-based evidence given unique circumstances |
| Growth as a leader | Developing positive self-efficacy by interacting and observing colleagues who persist with a successful implementation |

## SUMMARY

Leaders need to continually make discoveries about themselves to be able to make wise decisions as they navigate through the turbulence of a complex and rapidly changing educational environment. Every decision and action is an opportunity to learn—from the errors, the failures, and the successes. Leaders gradually and continually learn about themselves as learning leaders. They reflect on the development of ideas, capacities and practices, knowledge, and performances to help envision what might come next.

Leaders gradually develop the wisdom to know how to manage themselves in a variety of situations. In an agile organization, there is consistency throughout the school culture. The same patterns of behaviors that define an agile organization would be apparent in every dimension of the school system—from classroom to school, district, and the entire community—as a fractal quality. A fractal is a never-ending complex pattern that repeats itself across several levels of scale.

These five dispositions of leadership not only guide the work of the leadership of an organization but also are found in each of the components of the school. The dispositions are appropriate for the district leadership, the school leadership, and the classroom as well.

The five dispositions of leadership serve as a framework or schema for ongoing leadership development, school leadership teams, and the culture of the classroom. Educational leadership is unique due to both this fractal quality and the fact that, as stated in the introductory chapters of this book, leadership influences learning throughout the organization. This means creating a consistent culture of communication, curiosity, consciousness, collaboration, creativity, and continuous learning.

Leaders make, monitor, and sustain the commitment to consciously and intentionally use these five dispositions of leadership as a basis for effective thinking, communicating, and collaborating throughout the system. These dispositions are pivotal to success in being able to handle the complexity of challenges, problems, and tasks in the school and community.

## MIDDLE SCHOOL VIGNETTE

Fifteen school districts formed a leadership community to support school leaders and share resources. The district leaders recognized the need to provide support for principals due to high turnover rates and their inability to address complex problems in isolation. The districts formed a networked leadership community. A networked leadership community is a facilitated experience comprising high-performing teams of three or four principals who self-organize by implementation topic or similar school configuration.

The entire leadership community meets face-to-face for two days, three times per year, in high-performing teams. One major theme for the year was exploring and implementing feedback for *student and adult* learning and growth in high-performing teams by participating in a networked leadership community.

Nine middle-school principals from three high-performing teams decided that providing feedback to teachers in a skillful manner would influence how teachers in turn provide feedback to their students. The principals had participated in state-sponsored training for the collection of data during teacher observations. They were not convinced that feedback from observations was useful to promote professional growth for teachers.

The principals also acknowledged that feedback, provided to students and thoughtfully delivered with precision by teachers, is recognized as influencing student learning in a positive direction. The middle-school principals were alerted to the importance of feedback by the work of John Hattie (2009). The three teams of principals decided that reading and discussing effective feedback literature is more powerful when modeled during interactions with teachers. The principals decided to work together and share their expertise and resources around the goal of feedback for adults and students.

Two of the three teams, or six principals, were from middle schools in the same district, and the third team comprised principals from the only middle schools within their respective rural school districts. The facilitated networked leadership community, as a part of the commitment for participation by each high-performing team, had introduced "Networked Leadership Community Essential Characteristics" (table 7.4) and "Conditions that Promote Agility" (table 9.1).

The three teams had met face-to-face four times throughout the previous two years and also met by using web-based technology for ninety minutes every two to three weeks. The three teams had utilized the following material from the five dispositions of leadership that had been taught at the face-to-face meetings: a pervasive focus on student learning (textbox 4.1), seven norms of collaborative work (table 5.3), elements of dialogue, and the rehearsal conversation protocol (figure 5.1) when introducing new information to the staff.

The three high-performing teams decided to share the workload for designing a systematic approach for using feedback with teachers and students during a web-based meeting. Team one volunteered to examine and select multiple readings about teacher feedback with students by John Hattie (2009) and Dylan Wiliam (2011), as well as to identify several protocols that promote dialogue for use at faculty, grade-level, or department meetings. It was agreed during the web-based meeting that gathering information in each school about the current level of teacher practice using feedback was needed.

Team two volunteered to develop questions for all three teams using the attributes of high-quality questions (table 6.4) and reviewing the samples of high-quality questions (table 6.5). Team three volunteered to share examples of feedback having utilized table 7.3, "Attributes of Feedback for Adult Learning and Growth," as part of their teacher evaluation system training. They mentioned to team one and to team two that they had developed examples and nonexamples of providing feedback to teachers. Team three shared "Principal Feedback: Practice-Based Evidence" (table 9.2).

Team three suggested that a similar format could be developed as a starting point so that teachers could modify nonexamples into examples of effective feedback statements. The three teams discussed the merits of sharing with teachers their willingness to adjust and modify how a principal delivers feedback to teachers. The principals' school districts had all indicated that feedback as a formative assessment practice, techniques to increase student engagement, and feedback for teachers were goal priorities.

The three teams developed a "Goal Statement with action plans and action steps" (table 9.3) that included the work district leaders were hoping the principals would accomplish during the current school year. It was decided that a timeline would be established by each principal for his or her school because of other implementation topics in place currently and the flexibility needed due to the circumstances in each school district and

**Table 9.2.   Principal feedback: practice-based evidence**

| Feedback for adult learning and growth | Nonexample | Example |
|---|---|---|
| Specific | It seemed that lots of students kept asking for adjustments to the completion date for the assignment. | I observed two students at the end of fifth period world history requesting more time to complete the assignment due to unexcused absences. |
| Manageable | I noticed the students you assisted had many errors including run-on sentences, misspellings, comma faults, and noun/verb agreement on their American president paper. | I observed you review with two students the topic sentence and the first two paragraphs of the description of an American president for clarity and noun/verb agreement. |
| Factual | It looked as if the geography report you scored was good because the student followed the instructions for the assignment. | I heard the feedback to the student when you stated, "There are three examples (pages 3, 4, and 6) in your geography report where you cited evidence from text and met one requirement for the assignment." |
| Alterable | The student seems to have a bad attitude and does not like working with the other students in the life science class. | I observed during cooperative learning time in the life science class a student interrupt others on three occasions and talk over the speaker while elevating her voice. |

school. The principals agreed that the goal they had established with action plans and steps would be a focus of work during the second semester of the current year.

The three high-performing teams decided to meet separately as frequently as their busy schedules allowed. Each team of three principals committed to meet four times for ninety minutes during the second semester and to post information online that could be used by colleagues. One team had volunteered to take notes during the current meeting and developed the beginning of an online template (table 9.4) so the *new resources* that were created could be organized and aligned with resources they had already used.

The principals wanted to introduce the role of feedback in the learning process and felt modeling feedback in public with their teachers displayed

**Table 9.3. Goal Statement with action plans and action steps**

| Goal | Increase the use of effective feedback by principals and teachers to influence student and adult learning and growth. |
|---|---|
| Action plan | Action steps |
| Increase knowledge, awareness, and use of effective feedback with teachers. | Use and model the seven norms of collaborative work (table 5.3) in all meetings to promote thoughtful interactions between adults. |
| | Identify and use two protocols for using dialogue as a tool for reviewing professional readings. |
| | Review the literature with school leadership team, and identify key concepts, techniques, and ideas about feedback. |
| | Introduce to all staff members professional literature about the effective uses of feedback by John Hattie (2009) and Dylan Wiliam (2011), and provide timeline for all groups to complete. |
| | As a full staff at a faculty meeting, and in small groups by content area, identify the opportunities that are available during lessons to provide informative and descriptive feedback. |
| Model and improve the uses of feedback as school leaders. | Publicly share with teachers the attributes of effective feedback that principals will be attempting to model. |
| | During formal and informal meetings with teachers, model effective feedback. |
| | Develop with school leadership team and then distribute high-quality questions to gauge knowledge and uses by teachers of effective feedback in daily practice. |
| | Develop feedback protocol for teachers to use during peer-to-peer observations. (The two high-performing teams from the same district are using peer observation.) |
| | During classroom walkthroughs, collect examples of effective feedback used by teachers. |

**Table 9.4. Resources available for use by high-performing teams**

| | |
|---|---|
| **Thinking and acting interdependently (chapter 4)** | Textbox 4.1. Example of a shared vision based on a belief and one goal |
| **Communicating to influence (chapter 5)** | Table 5.3. The seven norms of collaboration |
| | Figure 5.1. Rehearsal conversation protocol |
| **Gathering and applying information for change (chapter 6)** | Table 6.4. Attributes of high-quality questions |
| | Textbox 6.1. Sample high-quality questions |
| **Seeking support and feedback for learning (chapter 7)** | Table 7.3. Attributes of feedback for adult learning and growth |
| | Table 7.4. Networked leadership community essential characteristics |
| | Table 7.5. Sample goal statement with action plans and action steps |
| **Discovering leadership potential in an agile organization (chapter 9)** | Table 9.1. Conditions that promote agility |
| | Table 9.2. Principal feedback: practice-based evidence |
| | Table 9.3. Goal statement with action plans and action steps |

a *high-stakes* method. It was suggested that a rehearsal conversation (figure 5.1) could be arranged with one other colleague as needed. All principals reiterated their professional commitment to one another, and support was a text message, an e-mail, or a phone call away.

## QUESTIONS TO ENGAGE YOUR THINKING AND DISCUSSION WITH COLLEAGUES

The following set of questions is a self-inventory to help you discover your "dispositional self." How skillfully, consistently, and deliberately do you

1. enhance the skills and talents of others?
2. call upon your values and dispositions rather than expediencies to guide decisions?
3. foster a vision and sense of mission in others in your organization?
4. express your curiosity? Sense of humor? Gratitude?
5. invite and show appreciation for feedback from others?
6. perceive the world through the lens of others?
7. respond to failures, dead ends, ambiguities, and disappointments as learning opportunities?
8. contribute to and build leadership capacities in others?
9. express optimism and positivity over negativism and defeat?
10. involve others in decision making?
11. listen with empathy, ask powerful questions, and make observations that will help others figure it out on their own?
12. Contemplate what's next in your own development?
13. observe not only yourself in action but also simultaneously how others respond to you?
14. seek frequent feedback about specific skills you wish to refine?
15. seek balanced feedback from all members of the staff or community?
16. reflect on the feedback from others as well as what you've observed about yourself?

Other questions to engage your thinking include:

1. What do you feel passionate about?
2. What do you most yearn for?
3. What do you dream about for your organization?
4. What motivates you about teaching and learning?

5. What drives you to act in the behalf of others?
6. About what are you curious?
7. Where in the educational spectrum do you derive your greatest pleasures?
8. Under what circumstances do you feel most virtuous and proud?
9. What brings you to tears?

## REFERENCES

Donaldson, G. (2008). *How leaders learn: Cultivating capacities for school improvement.* New York: Teachers College Press.

Hattie, J. (2009). *Visible learning: A synthesis of over 800 meta-analyses relating to achievement.* New York: Routledge.

Sutton, R., Hornsey, M. J., and Douglas, K. M. (Eds.). (2011). *Feedback: The communication of praise, criticism, and advice.* New York: Lang.

Wiliam, D. (2011). *Embedded formative assessment.* Bloomington, IN: Solution Tree Press.

# INDEX

# ABOUT THE AUTHORS

**Gary Whiteley** has been an educator for thirty-six years. He has served in many roles at the school level and district level, including classroom teacher, assistant principal, school principal, and assistant superintendent. He was a research associate with the Center for Research and Evaluation at the University of Maine and participated in program evaluations and research studies in New England. Whiteley was introduced to principal professional development by Gordon Donaldson and Roland Barth through the International Network of Principals' Centers at Harvard University.

Whiteley has served in numerous capacities for the Alaska Department of Education and Early Development. He was the director of the Alaska Administrator Coaching Project for ten years. He participated on the Technical Review Committee for the Alaska State Large-Scale Assessment System for five years. He cofounded Metis Education Consultants with colleague Lexie Domaradzki. The Metis team provides state-, district-, and school-level technical and professional development support.

**Lexie Domaradzki**'s primary areas of expertise are early childhood and kindergarten through grade 12 literacy, with emphases on research-based instruction for beginning readers and school reform. Currently Domaradzki is the owner of REACH Education consulting and provides technical assistance to state departments and districts in the area of leadership, RTI, assessment, and literacy. Prior to this work, she served as a research associate at RMC Research. Domaradzki provided technical assistance on the implementation of Reading First grants to the Northwest State Cluster Team for the National Reading Technical Assistance Center.

Prior to joining RMC Research, Domaradzki served as the assistant superintendent of teaching and learning for the Washington State Office of Superintendent of Public Instruction. Primary areas of responsibility included managing kindergarten through grade 12 content standards and supporting effective instructional practices for reading, mathematics, science, social studies, art, health and fitness, and early learning. During this time, she worked actively with legislators, the governor's office, the state board of education, and large education organizations to review policy and make recommendations.

**Arthur L. Costa** is an emeritus professor of education at California State University, Sacramento. He is cofounder of the Institute for Habits of Mind and cofounder of the Center for Cognitive Coaching. He has served as a classroom teacher, a science consultant for the Los Angeles County Superintendent of Schools Office, an assistant superintendent for instruction for the Sacramento County Office of Education, and as the director of educational programs for the National Aeronautics and Space Administration. He has made presentations and conducted workshops in all fifty states as well as on six of the seven continents.

Costa has written and edited numerous books, including *Techniques for Teaching Thinking* (with Larry Lowery) and *Cognitive Coaching* (with Bob Garmston). He is author of *The School as a Home for the Mind*; editor of *Developing Minds: A Resource Book for Teaching Thinking*; coeditor of the *Process as Content* trilogy (with Rosemarie Liebmann); coeditor with Bena Kallick of *Learning and Leading with Habits of Mind* and *Habits of Mind across the Curriculum*; and coauthor with Bena Kallick of *Assessment Strategies for Self-Directed Learning* and *Dispositions: Reframing Teaching and Learning*. His books have been translated into Arabic, Chinese, Italian, Spanish, and Dutch.

Active in many professional organizations, Costa served as president of the California Association for Supervision and Curriculum Development and was the national president of the Association for Supervision and Curriculum Development, from 1988 to 1989. He was the recipient of the Lifetime Achievement Award from the National Urban League in 2010 and the Malcolm Knowles Award for Lifelong Contributions to Self-Directed Learning from the International Society for Self-Directed Learning, 2017.

**Patricia Muller** is the director of research and evaluation at Indiana University's Center for Evaluation and Education Policy (CEEP), where she also serves as the center's executive associate director. She has served as the principal investigator and project director for more than twelve million dollars in funded research and evaluation, including large-scale international-, national-, regional-, and state-level work in the field of education. She has worked on projects across diverse content areas, including numerous research and evaluation projects related to school leadership such as the following: conducting a statewide evaluation of the Alaska Administrator Coaching Program (AACP); working closely and collaboratively with the U.S. ED Office of Innovation and Improvement (OII) at the U.S. Department of Education to provide comprehensive evaluation technical assistance (TA) for grantees within multiple programs, including the School Leadership Program; developing professional growth systems for the Idaho Network of Innovative School Leaders; and developing a performance evaluation rubric system for school administrators. Other work includes developing a theoretical framework for joint evaluation (collaboration) for the North Atlantic Treaty Organization (NATO); leading two Institute of Education Sciences (IES), U.S. Department of Education, randomized, controlled trial (RCT) studies; designing and implementing a comprehensive evaluation of a Race-to-the-Top grant; and directing a statewide evaluation of Reading First for the Ohio Department of Education.